RENTING OUR MINDS

How India Pays Thirty Billion Dollars a Year to Think on Foreign Infrastructure

Sivakumar Gingee

PEAQLABS

2026

Published by Peaqlabs.

ISBN: [to be assigned]

First edition, 2026.

The figures in this book are presented as ranges, with methodology stated, because honest uncertainty is more useful than false precision. The full methodology, source documentation, and data tables appear in Appendix A and in the accompanying research paper published by Peaqlabs.

}

Dedication

For the freedom fighters of India —

*who won the nation's freedom so it could govern itself,
and could not have foreseen that sovereignty would one day
have to be won again, in a territory without borders.*

This book is for them, and for that unfinished work.

"A nation that cannot govern its own data cannot fully govern itself."

Contents

Foreword

Some books arrive to tell us something we did not know. A rarer kind arrives to tell us how much we already knew without ever having counted it. *Renting Our Minds* is the second kind, which is both the harder thing to write and the more useful thing to read.

The condition at the centre of this book is not, on its face, a discovery. That India conducts much of its digital life on foreign infrastructure is known to anyone who has paid a cloud invoice, scrolled an advertising-funded feed, or clicked past a terms-of-service page written to be clicked past. What has been missing is not awareness but arithmetic. We have had the anecdote for two decades. We have not had the number. This book supplies it, and in doing so it changes the nature of the conversation — because a grievance can be dismissed, but an account must be answered.

I want to say a word, as someone trained in business and economics, about how that account is built, because it is the part most likely to be skimmed and the part that most deserves attention. The author does not give us a single, satisfying figure and ask for our trust. He gives us a range, category by category, with the method stated and the sources named, and he insists on using the conservative floor for the headline. This is the discipline of someone who would rather be defensibly approximate than impressively wrong. The most uncertain category — the value of data itself, for which no invoice has ever been written — is also the one he treats most cautiously, conceding openly that it cannot be measured directly and inviting the reader who distrusts it to set it aside entirely. That candour is not a weakness in the argument. It is the signature of serious work. The case survives even its own most skeptical reading.

The book also reaches, whether or not it announces the lineage, into some of the oldest and most fruitful ideas in economics. The observation that a country can export a raw material cheaply and buy it back dear as a finished good is older than this century; the structural economists of the post-war decades built a literature on it. What *Renting Our Minds* does is recognise that the pattern has quietly reassembled itself in software — that data is the new raw commodity, that the model trained on it is the new finished good, and that the margin between them is once again being captured somewhere other than where the material was grown. So too with the analysis of lock-in and network effects, and with the venerable understanding that some forms of infrastructure are public goods whose social value will always exceed what any private actor will pay to build them. None of this is invoked to show learning. It is invoked because it is the correct toolkit, and the author has had the good sense to pick it up.

Two further things distinguish the book from the genre it might have belonged to. The first is its refusal of victimhood. It would have been easy, and popular, to write an indictment of Silicon Valley. The author declines. He insists that the companies receiving the transfer built things India wanted and priced them at rates India accepted, and that the responsibility for the resulting dependency is therefore India's own. This is the less comfortable claim, and it is the more useful one, because a problem you caused is a problem you can solve. The second is the human architecture. The decision to carry an argument about balance-of-payments accounting on the shoulders of three ordinary people — a teacher, a founder, a farmer — is not a decorative choice. It is an analytical one. It keeps the reader's attention fixed on the truth that aggregates are made of individuals, and that no individual in this story did anything foolish.

The dependency is the sum of a billion sensible decisions. That is precisely why it cannot be solved one decision at a time, and why a book, rather than a budget line, is the right instrument to begin with.

What gets measured gets managed; what stays uncounted stays ungoverned. For a generation, this particular flow has stayed uncounted, not because anyone hid it but because no institution was ever asked to add it up. This book asks. It does so at a moment when the asking still matters — while the architecture of the next economic era is being poured and has not yet set. A few years from now, the same questions will still be worth posing, but the answers will be more expensive to act upon. That timing, more than any single figure, is the reason to read it now.

I do not agree with every estimate in these pages, and the author would be the first to say that exact agreement is not the point; the ranges are wide on purpose, and the argument is built to hold across them. What I agree with entirely is the proposition the book is finally about, stated plainly in its own epigraph: that a nation which cannot govern its own data cannot fully govern itself. That is not a technological claim. It is a claim about sovereignty, which is what nations are for — and it is the right claim for this moment in India's second century.

Ramganesh Subramanian

Doctorate in Business Administration, Swiss School of Business and Management

Delhi, 2026

Preface

I did not set out to write a book. I set out to find a number, and the book exists because the number was not there.

It began with a figure I had seen quoted my whole adult life and never questioned: the sum the world pays India for its software and services, announced each year with justified pride. One afternoon, for no reason I can reconstruct, I found myself wondering about the other direction. If we keep such careful track of what the world pays us, surely we keep equal track of what we pay the world. I went looking for that second number, expecting to find it in an afternoon. I did not find it that afternoon, or that month. After a while I understood that I was not failing to locate the number. The number had never been assembled. The advertising was counted in one place, the cloud spending in another, the app-store fees in a third, the data nowhere at all, and no institution had ever been asked to add the columns together. The silence, not the sum, was the surprise.

So I began to add the columns myself, and that work became this book. I want to be honest about the nature of that work, because the honesty is the only thing that makes the result worth anything. Some of these figures are firm, drawn straight from disclosures and official statistics. Others are estimates, and one of them — the value of the data we give away, which may be the most important of all — cannot be measured directly at all and had to be reasoned toward with deliberate caution. I have presented everything as a range rather than a point, and I have leaned, everywhere, toward the conservative end. I would much rather hand you a figure you can trust at its floor than one you would be right to doubt at its peak. Where I have guessed, I have said so. The method is laid out plainly enough that anyone who distrusts my arithmetic can redo it with their own.

I should say what this book is not, because the subject invites two misreadings and I would like to head off both. It is not an attack on the companies that receive the money. They built remarkable things, and the people in this country who use them — including me — use them because they are good. And it is not a lament. I have no interest in adding to the literature of grievance, which is large and accomplishes little. India does not appear in these pages as a victim. It appears as the one nation with almost everything required to do something about its situation, and most of the book is concerned not with the cost but with the opportunity, which I have come to believe is larger than the cost by a wide margin.

What moved me to keep going, through the unglamorous labour of reconciling estimates, was a conviction that grew rather than faded as the work went on: that this is, at bottom, a question about sovereignty, and therefore a question worthy of a citizen's attention rather than only a specialist's. The generation before mine won the freedom to govern this country. It did not occur to them, because it could not have, that an essential part of governing a country would one day mean governing the invisible flows of data and computation on which its economy had come to depend. That is the work that has fallen to us. I wanted to describe it clearly enough that it could be seen, and then to argue, as concretely as I could manage, that it can be done.

A book like this is necessarily a snapshot of a moving thing. Some of my numbers will be out of date by the time you read them; the direction they point will not be. I have tried to write something that will still be useful when the specifics have shifted, because the structure beneath the specifics changes slowly, and it is the structure I am really writing about.

I am grateful to more people than I can name here, and to a few I will name in the acknowledgements. Whatever is right in these pages, I owe in large part to them. Whatever is wrong is mine. My hope is modest and, I think, achievable: that you finish this book seeing something you could not see before, and that having seen it, you find you cannot quite unsee it. That is where every choice begins.

Sivakumar Gingee

2026

A NOTE ON THE NUMBERS AND THE PEOPLE

Two honesties are owed to the reader before the argument begins.

The first concerns the numbers. The figures in this book are drawn from the first comprehensive digital balance of payments ever constructed for India — built from corporate financial disclosures, industry analyst data, government publications, and international economic research. They are presented as ranges, not single points, because the honest answer to "how much does India pay to think on foreign infrastructure?" is a band, not a decimal. Where a number is contested, the book uses the conservative floor. Where a number cannot be sourced precisely, the book says so. The full methodology, the category-by-category construction, and the source documentation are set out in Appendix A, so that any reader who distrusts a figure can check the working rather than take it on faith. False precision would have been easier to write and worse to defend. The intention throughout is that a skeptical economist and a busy minister could both pick up the book, turn to the appendix, and find the receipts.

The second concerns the people. Priya, Arjun, and Suman, the three Indians whose mornings open this book and recur throughout it, are composites. Their specific details — the school in Coimbatore, the startup in Bangalore, the four acres in Ludhiana — are invented. Their situations are not. There are hundreds of millions of Priyas, tens of thousands of Arjuns, and hundreds of millions of Sumans, and every choice the three of them make in these pages is a choice that their real circumstances make rational. The book has no argument with any of them. Its argument is with the structure their choices have built. That distinction — between the person and the structure — is the whole moral architecture of what follows, and it is worth holding onto from the first page.

PROLOGUE

The Tide

Begin above it.

Not with one person, but with all of them at once. It is 7:14 in the morning in Coimbatore, and it is also 7:14 in Ludhiana, in Bengaluru, in Guwahati and Kochi and Indore and ten thousand towns whose names never reach a headline. The subcontinent is waking the way it always does, unevenly, by light and by habit, and as it wakes it reaches — five hundred million hands, more or less in the same hour, for the same small rectangle of glass.

Imagine you could see data the way a satellite sees weather. Imagine the country at dawn rendered not in land and water but in flows: every search a thread, every scroll a pulse, every photograph uploaded and every voice note sent a point of light leaving the place that made it. From that height you would not see chaos. You would see a pattern, steady and enormous, with a direction. You would see the light pooling for an instant over a village in Punjab or a flat in Salem, and then moving — outward, eastward and westward, off the edges of the map, toward a handful of buildings on the far side of two oceans where the pattern is gathered, stored, and turned into something worth more than it was when it left.

It looks, from up there, like a tide. And like a tide it goes out every morning, on schedule, without anyone deciding that it should.

No alarm sounds, because nothing is being stolen. Every thread of light was given freely, in exchange for something real — a message delivered, an answer found, a face seen across a distance that used to be uncrossable. The tide is not a crime. It is a transaction so vast and so distributed that no single party to it can feel its size, the way no single drop of water feels the ocean it belongs to.

It has been going out like this, morning after morning, for twenty years. Long enough that a generation has grown up never having seen the shore at low water. Long enough that the buildings on the far side of the oceans have learned the rhythm of an Indian day better than most Indians have ever been asked to think about it. And in all that time, across all those mornings, the one thing that has never happened is the simplest: no one has stood on the shore with a ledger and counted what goes out.

Now come down.

Down through the height, through the cloud layer and the pattern and the flows, until the country resolves again into land and water, and the land into a city, and the city into a street, and the street into a single lit window where a woman is awake before her family because the quiet of the morning is the only thing in the day that is entirely hers. She has a phone in her hand. She is running late. She has no idea that she is part of the tide, or that there is a tide at all, and there is no reason on earth that she should.

Her name is Priya, and this book begins with her.

It begins by teaching you to see the tide — the size of it, the direction of it, the machinery beneath it. And then it asks the only question that finally matters: whether a nation that can watch its wealth go out with every morning will decide, at last, to build a shore.

INTRODUCTION

The Number Nobody Adds Up

India keeps careful track of what the world pays it.

Every year, the Reserve Bank of India and the Ministry of Electronics and Information Technology publish the figure that India is rightly proud of: the value of the software and technology services that Indian companies sell to the rest of the world. In the most recent fiscal year it was roughly two hundred and five billion dollars — the dividend on four decades of investment in engineering education and the historical accident that made India the back office of the global digital economy. It is one of the most-cited numbers in Indian public life, and it deserves to be.

India does not keep track of the reverse.

There is no line, in any official document, for what India pays foreign technology companies for the infrastructure on which its own digital life now runs. Not because the spending is hidden — it is itemized in ten thousand corporate ledgers and a billion credit-card statements — but because it is scattered across so many categories and so many institutions that no single body has ever been asked to add it up. The advertising that funds the platforms. The cloud bills that keep the startups alive. The software subscriptions that run every office. The app-store commissions, the payment-rail fees, the hardware royalties. And, beneath all of it, uncounted in any currency, the data — the behavioural and cognitive raw material that five hundred million Indians generate every day and give away for free.

This book adds it up. The number, constructed category by category in Part Two and documented in Appendix A, has a conservative floor of about **thirty-three billion dollars a year** in money that leaves India, plus an estimated ten to thirty billion dollars a year in data value that no invoice has ever captured. The midpoint of the full range is close to forty-eight billion dollars. Whichever end of the band you trust, the figure is large, it is recurring, it is growing at thirty to forty per cent a year in its fastest categories, and it has never appeared on any balance sheet that India publishes.

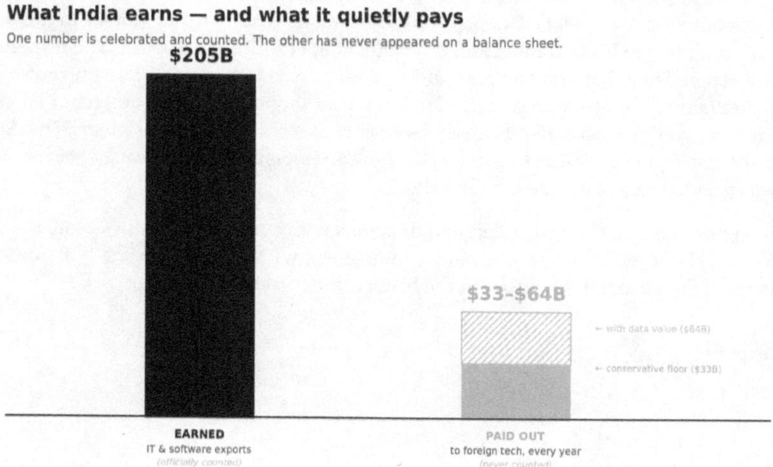

Figure 1. India's digital balance of payments, in one image. Sources: RBI, Appendix A

That is the discovery. The rest of the book is what to do about it.

The argument runs in six movements.

See it. Part One follows three ordinary Indians through three ordinary mornings and shows the transfer operating in the background of a scroll, a cloud bill, and a crop search. Nothing in their behaviour is foolish. That is the point.

Understand the architecture. Part Two follows the money through all seven categories, constructs the thirty-three-billion-dollar floor, and then shows why the dependency is not an accident that can be fixed by individuals making better choices. It is a trap that sets itself — economically, through switching costs; jurisdictionally, through terms of service no one reads; and temporally, because every year of delay makes the next year harder.

Learn from those who tried. Part Three studies the four nations that confronted a version of this problem — China, the European Union, South Korea, Estonia — and extracts from each a lesson India can use and a mistake India must avoid. None of their answers can be copied wholesale. All of them are instructive.

Count what India already has. Part Four is the turn most accounts of this subject miss. India is not a victim in this story; it is the one nation on earth with the scale, the talent, the diplomatic position, and the proven digital public infrastructure to build a genuine alternative. UPI, Aadhaar, the Account Aggregator framework, ONDC — India has already done the hard thing once. The argument that it cannot build is over.

See the prize. Part Five describes what winning looks like: not walls, not the eviction of foreign technology, but Indian digital infrastructure good enough to choose on its merits, governed by Indian law, and offered to the three billion people in the Global South who are looking for a third option that is neither American nor Chinese.

Make the choice. Part Six turns the whole argument into fifteen specific decisions, sorted by time horizon, each with its objection answered — and then shows, in two honest extrapolations of the year 2047, what India looks like at one hundred years old depending on whether those decisions are made.

A word on what this book is not. It is not an indictment of the companies that receive the thirty-three billion dollars. Meta, Google, Amazon, and Microsoft are not villains in this accounting; they built things India wanted and priced them at rates India accepted. The responsibility for the dependency that grew up around those services is Indian — a more uncomfortable truth than blaming Silicon Valley, and a far more useful one, because a problem you caused is a problem you can solve. Nor is this book a work of technological pessimism. The dependency is the consequence of decisions, which is the most hopeful thing that can be said about it. What was decided can be decided differently.

It begins, though, not with a decision. It begins with a schoolteacher in Coimbatore, reaching for her phone at 7:14 in the morning, running late, with no idea that she is about to take part in the largest economic transfer in the history of her country.

PART ONE

THE USERS

Who We Think We Are

Before there is an argument, there are three people. They have not met and never will. They live a thousand kilometres apart and occupy different centuries of the same country at the same moment in time. What they share is a small rectangle of glass and the fact that none of them has been told what it is doing on their behalf.

This part of the book asks for nothing except attention. No alarm, no conclusions, no policy. Just three mornings, watched closely enough that the architecture becomes visible underneath them.

CHAPTER ONE

7:14 AM, Coimbatore

Priya opens Instagram at 7:14 in the morning.

She is a schoolteacher in Coimbatore, thirty-one years old, up before her husband and her daughter because the morning is the only time the flat is quiet and she has learned to protect it. The phone is the first thing she reaches for, not because she is addicted to it, though she might be, but because it is the fastest way to know whether anything happened while she slept. Whether her mother called. Whether school has a circular. Whether the news is bad in the particular way that requires her to prepare.

She scrolls for eleven minutes. A cousin's wedding photograph. A recipe she will save and never make. A news video she watches for forty seconds before skipping. A reel from a brand selling kajal that makes her pause, and then tap, and then close the tab when she sees the price. Two messages from the school parents' group that do not require a response. A video of a child dancing that makes her smile and which the algorithm registers as a prolonged engagement and stores as a data point in a file that will be used to show her more dancing children and more kajal and more things that are priced just above what she will pay.

That pause — the three seconds she lingers on the kajal before deciding it is too expensive — is the most valuable thing she does all morning, and it is the one thing she does not know she is doing. It is recorded with more precision than she records it herself. Not only that she looked, but for how long, and after what, and before what, and at what hour of which day in what sequence of moods. A profile that has been accumulating since she first installed the app understands her price sensitivity better than she could articulate it. The next kajal advertisement she sees will be cheaper, or framed as a discount, or timed to her salary date, because the system has learned the exact distance between what she wants and what she will pay, and its entire purpose is to close that distance by a rupee at a time. She experiences this as the app "knowing her." It is more accurate to say the app has been *paid* to know her, by people she will never see, in a currency she never agreed to spend.

By 7:25, she puts the phone down and starts the coffee.

She does not know that in those eleven minutes, she has contributed to a transfer of approximately forty-two rupees to a company incorporated in Delaware, headquartered in Menlo Park, California, listed on the NASDAQ, and worth well over a trillion dollars. She does not know that this happens every morning, to her and to five hundred million other Indians, and that the aggregate of all these 7:14 moments across all these Indian mornings amounts to somewhere between thirty-three thousand and forty-two thousand crore rupees flowing out of India every year. She does not know that this number has never appeared on any official balance sheet, that no Indian minister has been asked to account for it, and that no policy currently in force addresses it with any seriousness proportionate to its scale.

She just knows she is running late for school.

This book is about what Priya does not know.

It is about the thirty billion dollars, which is the part you can see if you know where to look. And it is about the additional ten to thirty billion dollars in behavioural data and cognitive raw material that India gives away freely every day, which is the part that is harder to see and, arguably, more consequential.

It is about the architecture of a transfer that was not designed by anyone and not chosen by anyone. It emerged from a billion rational individual decisions, each one entirely sensible, whose aggregate produced a dependency that no individual decision-maker would have chosen if they had been shown the collective result in advance.

It is about what four other nations did when they found themselves in comparable situations, and what India can learn from each of them without repeating their mistakes.

It is about what India already has, which is more than most Indians know.

And it is about what India could build, which is more than most Indians have been asked to imagine.

Before any of that, though, it is about Priya. And Arjun. And Suman.

Arjun runs a startup in Bangalore that connects small manufacturers with export buyers. He built it on Amazon Web Services in 2019 because AWS was what he knew, what his co-founder knew, what every bootcamp and tutorial and Stack Overflow thread pointed toward. He has twelve employees now and a product that works. He also has a technical architecture that would cost more to migrate than his last two years of AWS bills combined. He has no plan to migrate. The question has never come up in any investor meeting or board discussion. The infrastructure is simply there, the way the road outside his office is there, and he pays for it every month the way he pays for electricity: automatically, without thinking about whose hands the payment passes through on its way to the other side of the world.

Suman farms four acres of wheat in Ludhiana. He has a smartphone because his son set it up for him three years ago, and he uses it primarily for one thing: to ask Google what is wrong with his crop. He types in broken Hindi, sometimes with photographs, sometimes just with descriptions of what he is seeing: yellowing leaves, black spots, wilting at the stem. Google answers with some accuracy and enough confidence that he has stopped calling the agricultural extension office, which is three kilometres away and often unhelpful anyway. What Suman does not know, because why would he, is that his queries are contributing to a training dataset. That the specific way he describes his problem, the Hindi he uses, the agricultural vocabulary he reaches for, the symptoms he has learned to name over thirty years of farming, is valuable to the artificial intelligence systems that will, within a decade, become the primary interface between Indian farmers and information about their land. He is training the system that will eventually be sold back to him. The price he will pay for the intelligence he is currently generating for free has not yet been set. It will be higher than zero.

Priya. Arjun. Suman. Three people who have made entirely rational choices using the tools available to them, contributing without knowledge to the largest economic transfer in Indian history that no one is counting.

The transfer is not the result of bad decisions. It is the result of no decision at all. A billion individual choices, each sensible in isolation, whose aggregate produced a dependency that no one chose and no one is accountable for.

The first thing this book asks you to do is see it.

Not with alarm. Alarm is not useful here, and it is not honest. The platforms that Priya, Arjun, and Suman use are genuinely excellent. Instagram connects Priya to her cousins in a way that nothing before it made possible. AWS gave Arjun's startup capabilities that would have cost a hundred times as much a decade earlier. Google Search has made Suman a better farmer than he would have been without it. The value is real. The dependency is the problem, not the service — and the two have to be held in the mind at the same time, because any argument that forgets the first will be correctly ignored by the people who use these tools every day and know exactly how good they are.

The second thing this book asks you to do is understand the architecture.

The transfer from India to Silicon Valley is not random. It is structural. It follows the same logic in advertising and in cloud and in data and in software subscriptions and in app store fees. It operates through the same mechanism in every category: India generates the value, foreign companies capture it, and the capture compounds because the infrastructure that enables the capture is the same infrastructure India has built its digital economy on top of. It is a toll road where the toll collector also built the road and also owns the land and also, increasingly, is building the intelligence that will determine which trucks are allowed to use it.

The third thing this book asks you to do is consider what India has that nobody else does.

This is the part that most treatments of this subject get wrong. They treat India as a victim. India is not a victim. India is the one nation in the world that has, simultaneously, the scale to build alternatives at global significance, the engineering talent to build them well, the diplomatic position to make them trustworthy to nations that trust neither Washington nor Beijing, and the existing digital public infrastructure that proves it can be done. China did it behind walls. The European Union regulated without building. South Korea did it with industrial policy and a generation of patience. Estonia did it with one million people and exceptional architectural thinking. India has what none of them had. The question is whether India will use it.

Priya does not know any of this. She is already on the bus to school, checking her messages, the phone alive in her hand, the data flowing in both directions, the thirty-billion-dollar architecture operating in the background of every tap and scroll and search.

By the time you finish this book, you will see what she cannot see yet.

And you will understand why that matters.

CHAPTER TWO

The Startup Stack

Arjun does not think about his infrastructure the way he does not think about his spine.

It is there. It holds everything up. It works until it doesn't, at which point the problem becomes the only thing in the room. In the seven years since he started the company, it has never not worked. So he does not think about it. He thinks about his customers, his team, his burn rate, the manufacturer in Tirupur who missed a shipment window and the buyer in Stuttgart who is considering switching to a competitor in Bangladesh. He thinks about all the things that require active thinking. The infrastructure runs on its own, the way spines do, in the background of everything, reliably invisible.

He is thirty-four years old and he built his first production service on Amazon Web Services when he was twenty-seven, sitting in a flat in Koramangala with his co-founder Vikram and a laptop that overheated if you ran two browser tabs and a terminal simultaneously. The year was 2019. They were building a platform to connect India's small and mid-sized manufacturers with international buyers who wanted to source from India but had no efficient way to find and vet the right suppliers. The problem was real. The pain was real. They had both seen it: Arjun's uncle ran a garment unit in Salem, had been running it for twenty-two years, had excellent production capacity and international-standard quality, and had no way to reliably reach buyers beyond the three relationships he had inherited from his father.

So they built.

AWS was not a decision, exactly. It was an assumption, the way English is the assumption you write your pitch deck in. You could ask why they chose AWS over alternatives, but it would be like asking why they chose to write code. It was simply the medium that the world they inhabited was made of. Every tutorial they had followed, every bootcamp they had attended, every Stack Overflow thread they had spent evenings inside pointed toward the same set of services: EC2 for compute, RDS for the database, S3 for file storage, CloudFront for content delivery. The documentation was in English. The community was enormous. The pricing was comprehensible if you had time to study it, which they did, in the way that twenty-seven-year-olds with a borrowed idea and a real problem always find time for things that matter.

They signed up for an AWS account on a Tuesday. By Friday they had a working prototype.

That decision took eleven minutes.

Seven years later, Arjun has twelve employees and a product that processes around four hundred active supplier listings and serves sixty-three verified international buyers across eleven countries. Revenue is real. Growth is real. The platform works, not in a startup-speaking way where "works" means it does not crash, but in a fundamental business way where it creates value that people pay for. Suppliers get buyers they would never have found. Buyers get suppliers they can trust. Arjun takes a margin on the transaction. It is a clean model, honestly earned, built on a genuine insight about a structural gap in how Indian manufacturing connects to the world.

The infrastructure bill arrives every month from Amazon. Last year, across all their services, it came to approximately forty-two lakhs. Roughly fifty thousand US dollars. It is the second-largest line item after salaries. Arjun pays it the way he pays rent: automatically, without reviewing it, the way you do not read the fine print on the electricity bill.

He has thought, once, about migrating.

It was eighteen months ago. A friend who runs a competing platform mentioned over dinner that he had started moving some workloads to a smaller cloud provider and was saving around twenty per cent. Arjun asked a few questions. His CTO, Lakshmi, was on the call and she listened carefully and said she would look into it.

Three weeks later, Lakshmi came back with a number, and the number had a shape to it that Arjun recognised immediately as the shape of a closed door. A full migration to any alternative infrastructure would cost between seventy and ninety lakhs in engineering time, downtime risk management, and the rebuilding of all the service integrations they had accumulated over seven years. She walked him through it line by line. The database migration alone would take two engineers the better part of three months, during which they would not be building anything customers could see. The monitoring and alerting stack — the system that paged Lakshmi at 3 a.m. when something broke — was wired into AWS-specific services that had no clean equivalent and would have to be rebuilt from scratch and then trusted, which takes longer than building it. There were forty-one separate integrations, accumulated one reasonable decision at a time, and each one was a small migration of its own. At their current AWS spend, the total came to between one and a half and two years of infrastructure bills. And the savings at the end of it would not be certain.

They did not migrate.

The subject has not come up since.

What Arjun knows is that AWS is expensive relative to what it was when he started. What he knows is that the prices have increased three times in the years he has been a customer, each increase announced with thirty days' notice and absorbed without real alternative. What he knows is that the terms of service give AWS the right to change pricing with notice, to deprecate services with notice, to modify the technical specifications of what they are selling with notice, and that "notice" in all these cases means notification to an email address that his office manager monitors and that Arjun himself has not personally read in two years.

What he does not know is the direction the money flows.

Forty-two lakhs a year. Fifty thousand dollars, leaving India. Leaving his company, which is incorporated in Bangalore under Indian law, which has Indian employees paying Indian taxes, which generates economic activity in the Indian manufacturing sector, which is in every conventional sense of the word an Indian business. Fifty thousand dollars a year moving from this Indian business to a company incorporated in Delaware, headquartered in Seattle, listed on the NASDAQ, which pays taxes in the United States, which employs engineers in Virginia and Oregon and the greater Seattle metropolitan area, which counts Arjun's payment as American revenue.

Arjun is not the only one.

There are, depending on how you count and which registration database you consult, somewhere between eighty thousand and one hundred and twenty thousand active technology startups in India. The number changes constantly. A conservative estimate of average infrastructure spend for a company at Arjun's stage is somewhere between fifteen and forty lakhs per year. The vast majority of that spend goes to three companies: Amazon, Microsoft, and

Google. All American. All subject to American law, American regulatory authority, American foreign policy.

The total outflow from Indian startups alone, for cloud infrastructure, is somewhere between twelve thousand and thirty-five thousand crore rupees per year. Every year. Growing.

No one in Arjun's investor meetings has ever asked about it.

This is not because investors are incurious. Arjun has raised two rounds, from two firms, and he has been asked about his infrastructure in both of them. He has been asked whether his architecture can scale. He has been asked about his disaster recovery plan. He has been asked whether he is over-provisioned.

He has not been asked where the money goes.

The question that has never been asked, in any of his board meetings or investor calls or conversations with advisors, is the structural question: what does it mean for an Indian business to be built on American infrastructure, under American terms of service, subject to American export-control regulations, potentially affected by American sanctions policy?

It is not that anyone has decided these questions are unimportant. It is that no one has decided to ask them.

Lakshmi knows this, actually. She did the migration analysis and she noticed, while she was doing it, that their entire data layer lives on servers located in Singapore and Mumbai but governed by American law. The AWS customer agreement that Arjun signed in 2019, without reading, contains a clause that subjects data stored on AWS to the reach of US courts and to US government access requests under the CLOUD Act, regardless of where the servers are physically located.

She noted it. She did not know what to do with it. It was not a legal problem she could solve and not a technical problem she could solve and not a business problem that had an obvious next action. So she filed it in the part of her mind where things go when they are important but not urgent, which is the part of the mind where the most consequential things in a life are usually kept.

Arjun is not naïve and he is not lazy. He is a competent founder who has made reasonable decisions under realistic constraints and built something that works. The choice he made in 2019 was the right choice, given everything available to him in 2019. There was no Indian cloud provider with the reliability, the documentation, the community support, the service breadth, or the pricing structure that would have allowed him to build what he built on the timeline he built it.

The problem is not the decision he made. The problem is that no alternative existed to make a different decision with.

And the problem behind that problem is that no alternative will exist, not reliably, not at scale, unless someone builds it. Building it requires investment, which requires a belief that the market will exist, which requires founders choosing it, which requires it to be good enough to choose, which requires it to already exist.

This is a trap. It is not a trap that anyone set. It is the kind of trap that sets itself.

He is in a meeting now, on his laptop, the screen showing a video call with a buyer in Hamburg who is asking about lead times for the winter collection. Arjun is explaining that the supplier in Tirupur can turn around twelve hundred units in six weeks if the fabric specifications are locked by Thursday. The buyer says he will come back to him by end of week. Arjun thanks him and closes the laptop.

The AWS bill has been charged to the company credit card. The transaction settled in dollars. The dollars are in Seattle. Somewhere in the settlement, on the rupee leg of the conversion, a small fee went to an American card network too, which is a different chapter.

Arjun makes himself a coffee. He has three more calls before lunch.

CHAPTER THREE

What the Crop Knows

Suman is fifty-three years old and he has been reading his wheat for thirty years.

He learned from his father, who learned from his father, who farmed the same four acres outside Ludhiana in a Punjab that has changed so completely in the time between them that the only thing reliably continuous is the soil itself and the particular way wheat looks when it is under stress. Yellowing at the tips means something different from yellowing at the stem. Black spots in the second week after germination mean something different from black spots in the fifth. Wilting in the afternoon heat is one kind of problem. Wilting in the morning, before the sun is fully up, is a different kind entirely, the kind that means something has gone wrong underground where you cannot see it.

Suman can read all of these. He has been wrong about them, sometimes. He has also been right about them enough times that he trusts his reading more than he trusts the agricultural extension office, which is three kilometres away, which is run by a man who is technically qualified and practically unhelpful, who speaks in recommendations so generalised that they apply to every farm and therefore to none.

Three years ago, his son Kulwant set up a smartphone for him. Kulwant works in Chandigarh, comes home on alternate weekends, and worries about his father the way educated sons of farmers worry: with a combination of love and guilt and the specific anxiety of not knowing enough about farming to know what to worry about. The smartphone was partly practical and partly a way of feeling that Suman had access to something, resources of some kind, in the years when Kulwant could not be there.

It took Suman six months to find his way to Google.

Now he uses it every day.

The method is not elegant but it works. He types into the search bar in Hindi, slowly, using the transliteration keyboard that Kulwant showed him, which turns Roman letters into Devanagari in a way that still feels slightly miraculous. Sometimes he uses photographs, holding the phone close to the affected part of the plant, letting the camera focus, submitting the image to Google Lens and then reading what comes back. He cross-references between the search results and what he already knows, using thirty years of reading to filter what is useful from what is not. He is not naïve about the internet. He knows it contains wrong answers. He applies judgement.

The results are good enough. Better than the extension office. Better than calling his neighbour Harpal, who is a competent farmer but tends toward the same two explanations for every problem regardless of the symptoms. Better than waiting for the agricultural university's quarterly advisory, which arrives by mail, which is rarely timed to the actual problem. There is a quiet indignity in this that Suman feels but has never said aloud: the public institutions built to advise him — the extension office, the university, the cooperative — were funded by his country and staffed by his countrymen and they have been quietly out-competed, in the field where he stands, by a search engine built in California that never set out to advise an Indian farmer at all and does it better anyway, almost as a side effect.

Last March, Suman noticed something he had never seen before: a pale yellow streaking along the leaves of the wheat in his eastern plot, running vertically with the grain of the leaf rather than spreading out from a central point. He had not seen it in thirty years. He typed the description into Google. He added a photograph. Three results came back, two of them useless. The third was a research paper from Punjab Agricultural University that identified the streaking as a symptom of wheat streak mosaic virus, a disease spread by mites in conditions of late-sown crop and warm autumn temperatures, exactly the conditions of last autumn. The paper recommended removing and burning the affected plants to prevent spread.

He did that. He did not contact the extension office.

The virus was contained to the eastern plot. His yield loss was less than eight per cent.

There is an irony in the source that Suman will never register and that matters more than he could guess: the answer that saved his crop came from a paper written by an Indian university, about an Indian disease, in Indian conditions — and it reached him only because an American search engine had indexed it, ranked it, and surfaced it above two useless results. The knowledge was Indian. The infrastructure that delivered it was not. And the infrastructure kept a copy of the question.

Here is what Suman does not know.

He does not know that each query he submits — the Hindi text, the photograph, the implicit structure of how he describes what he sees — is being stored. Not maliciously. Not secretly, exactly: it is in the terms of service, which he did not read, which are available in English, which would not have been comprehensible to him even in Hindi because they are written in the particular form of legal language that is comprehensible only to people whose profession is reading legal language.

He does not know that the specific vocabulary he uses, the agricultural terms he has developed over thirty years, the Hindi idioms for crop diseases that do not have direct equivalents in English, the particular way he describes symptoms that he can see but cannot name precisely, is valuable. Not in the way that his neighbour Harpal's land is valuable. Valuable in the way that training data is valuable, which is a different kind of value: abstract, cumulative, and invisible.

He does not know that across Punjab, across Haryana, across the wheat-growing districts of Madhya Pradesh and Uttar Pradesh, millions of farmers like him are typing similar queries into similar search bars, submitting similar photographs, building collectively — without intention, without knowledge, without compensation — a dataset of Indian agricultural knowledge that did not exist in machine-readable form before the smartphone arrived in their hands. This is the crucial point, and it is the one most easily missed: the knowledge always existed, in the hands and eyes and memory of a hundred and fifty million farming households. What did not exist was a way to collect it. The smartphone is that way. Every query is a deposit into a vault that is being filled by Indians and owned by someone else.

He does not know that this dataset is being used to train the artificial intelligence systems that will, within the next decade, become the primary interface between Indian farmers and advice about their land.

He does not know what it will cost.

He knows the smartphone costs about three hundred rupees a month for the data plan. He pays it without thinking about it, the way you pay for water.

This is the part that requires the most careful description, because it is the part most likely to be misunderstood.

What is happening to Suman is not a theft. The word theft implies a moment of taking, a deliberate act, a thing that was yours and is now not yours. None of that is quite right here. Suman has lost nothing he had. He has gained something real: access to information that has made him a better farmer, that contained the specific knowledge about wheat streak mosaic virus that protected eight per cent of his yield last March. The value he received was genuine.

What has happened is something more complicated and, in some ways, more consequential than theft. It is extraction without transaction. Suman has contributed something — his knowledge, his agricultural vocabulary, his thirty years of pattern recognition encoded in the way he describes what he sees — to a system that is accumulating a resource of enormous future value, and he is not a party to any of the decisions about how that resource will be used, who will own it, how it will be priced, or whether the people who generated it will have any claim on the benefits it produces.

What makes the Suman case particular, what makes the Indian case particular, is scale and stakes. There are approximately one hundred and fifty million agricultural households in India. Each of them carries, the way Suman carries, a store of local agricultural knowledge accumulated across generations. This knowledge is being converted into data, at scale, in real time, by the simple act of farmers asking questions and receiving answers.

The intelligence that will govern Indian agriculture in 2035 is being built now, from this data, by companies that are not Indian, on servers that are not in India, under laws that are not Indian laws.

Suman is not an input to someone else's product. He is, in the precise technical sense, a training set.

The extension office called last month. There was a new advisory about a fungal risk in the district. Suman listened politely. He thanked the officer. He had already found the advisory on Google three days earlier, along with two research papers that gave him more detail than the extension office's summary.

He is grateful for the smartphone. Kulwant was right to set it up.

At no point in the conversation with the extension officer did Suman describe what he had found on Google or how he had found it. Not because he was hiding anything but because it did not seem relevant. He had solved the problem. The solution had come from a search. The search had cost him nothing except the data plan.

Priya is scrolling. Arjun is paying his cloud bill. Suman is outside now, walking the eastern plot, the one where the virus was last March, checking the new growth with his hands.

Three people. Three rational choices. Three contributions to a transfer that has no single author, no moment of decision, no obvious place to intervene.

This is what we are paying. This is where it goes.

Now we need to understand why.

PART TWO

THE ARCHITECTURE

What Is Actually Happening

Part One asked you to see three people. Part Two asks you to see the machine behind them.

The word *machine* is chosen carefully, because what follows is not a story about greed or conspiracy. It is a story about structure — about a set of flows that behave the same way in advertising as in cloud as in data, that compound rather than dissipate, and that were assembled, without a designer, into something that now functions with the regularity of plumbing. The first task is to follow the money until it adds up to a number. The second is to follow the money past the point where money is involved at all, into the data that no one invoices. The third is to explain why the whole arrangement holds itself in place. And the fourth is to ask the question that turns an economic problem into a sovereign one: when your country's digital life runs on someone else's infrastructure, whose law governs your mind?

CHAPTER FOUR

Following the Money

No one has done this accounting before.

That is not an exaggeration offered for dramatic effect. It is a factual description of a gap in the record. India's official balance of payments contains a category called "software and IT services" that records what Indian companies earn by selling technology to the world. It is a number India is rightly proud of: roughly two hundred and five billion dollars in the last fiscal year, the result of four decades of investment in engineering education and the particular historical accident that made India the back office of the global digital economy.

What the balance of payments does not contain, in any organized form, is the reverse. The column for what India *pays* foreign technology companies does not exist as a coherent entry. It is distributed across categories in ways that make the total invisible unless you go looking for it in a specific way that official accountants have not been asked to go looking for it.

So we will go looking for it now.

We will do it in categories, because that is the only honest way to do it. The number is not one payment. It is the aggregate of seven distinct flows, each with its own mechanism, its own logic, and its own rate of growth. Every figure that follows is constructed in full in Appendix A; here, the point is the shape of the thing.

Category One: Social media and search advertising. Meta — which owns Instagram, Facebook, and WhatsApp — is the largest single recipient of Indian digital advertising spend by most measures. Its India revenue runs to roughly four to five billion dollars a year, reconstructed from its regional disclosures and analyst estimates. Call it thirty-three to forty-two thousand crore rupees. Google takes a comparable sum again: its Indian advertising revenue is estimated at three to four billion dollars annually, and the fees it collects through the Play Store add several hundred million more. Between Meta and Google alone you are looking at seven to nine billion dollars a year leaving India before you have counted anything else. Every rupee of it is a rupee that an Indian advertiser — a kajal brand, a coaching institute, a fintech app — paid to reach an Indian consumer, routed through California.

Category Two: Cloud infrastructure. This is the number Arjun contributes to. Amazon Web Services, Microsoft Azure, and Google Cloud together serve the overwhelming majority of Indian enterprise and startup computing. The Indian cloud market was approximately six to eight billion dollars in the most recent year, and it is growing at thirty to forty per cent annually. On current trajectory it will be fifteen to twenty billion dollars by 2027. The bulk of that economic value flows to the American parent companies.

Category Three: Software subscriptions. Microsoft 365 is the dominant productivity suite across Indian enterprise, government, and education. Add Zoom, Teams, Slack, Adobe Creative Cloud, Salesforce, and the long tail of software-as-a-service tools that now run virtually every Indian business of any scale, and the total software-subscription outflow is somewhere between three and five billion dollars a year. Unlike a one-time licence, a subscription is a tap that never closes; it is the purest form of the rental relationship this book is named for.

Category Four: App store commissions. Google takes fifteen to thirty per cent of in-app purchases on Android; Apple takes the same on iOS. Across a market of seven hundred million smartphone users, these commissions aggregate to one to two billion dollars a year — a private toll collected on transactions between an Indian creator and an Indian consumer, by companies incorporated in the United States, on a road neither of them can avoid.

Category Five: Digital payments rails. When an Indian business pays a foreign vendor, or an Indian freelancer is paid by a foreign client, the transaction typically routes through SWIFT or through Visa, Mastercard, and PayPal. The fees, across the volume of India's international digital commerce, add up to roughly eight hundred million to one and a half billion dollars a year. (Domestically, as Part Four will show, UPI has already taken this category to near zero — proof that the leak is a choice, not a law of nature.)

Category Six: Hardware and semiconductor intellectual property. India manufactures almost none of the hardware on which its digital economy runs. The chips are Taiwanese and American, the displays South Korean, the operating systems Californian. A conservative estimate of the intellectual-property component of India's hardware import bill — the royalty, not the assembly — is five to eight billion dollars a year.

Category Seven: Data. This is the category that has never been counted, because the first six involve money changing hands and this one involves no invoice at all. No payment record. No accounting entry of any kind. What Suman does not know is that his crop queries have a value that has never been priced. The data that five hundred million Indian users generate daily is the raw material for the artificial-intelligence systems that will govern the next fifty years of economic activity. Using conservative methodology, the implied value of India's annual data contribution to foreign platforms is somewhere between ten and thirty billion dollars. We will use the floor: ten billion. An annual contribution — unpriced, uncompensated, unacknowledged in any balance-of-payments document.

The total.

Category	Annual outflow (USD)
1. Social media & search advertising	$7–9 billion
2. Cloud infrastructure	$6–8 billion
3. Software subscriptions	$3–5 billion
4. App store commissions	$1–2 billion
5. Digital payments fees	$0.8–1.5 billion
6. Hardware & semiconductor IP	$5–8 billion
7. Data (unpriced)	$10–30 billion
Total	**$33–64 billion**

Following the money: the seven flows

Each bar shows the low-high estimate. The book's headline adds only the lows: a $33B floor.

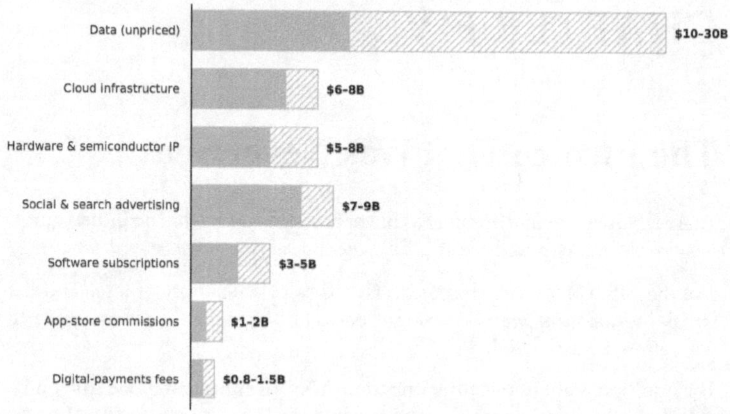

FLOOR (sum of lows) = $33B · midpoint of full range = $48B

Figure 2. Solid = conservative low estimate; hatched = upper range. Source: Appendix A.

The midpoint of this range is approximately forty-eight billion dollars. The midpoint of the first six categories — the money that demonstrably changes hands — is about twenty-two billion. The number most defensible as a conservative floor, using the low estimate for every category including data, is approximately **thirty-three billion dollars**.

Thirty-three billion dollars. Every year. Growing.

No single document in the Indian government's possession contains this number. No parliamentary committee has been asked to address it. No ministry publishes an annual report on it. MeitY publishes India's IT export growth; the Ministry of Finance publishes the balance of payments; neither has, to this author's knowledge, ever published the aggregate outflow to foreign technology companies constructed in these pages. The number is not hidden. It is distributed across too many places for any single institution to have had occasion to add it up.

This book is adding it up.

A word on what this number is *not*. It is not an indictment of the companies that receive it. Meta, Google, Amazon, and Microsoft built things India wanted and priced them at rates India found acceptable. The responsibility for the structural dependency that grew up around those services is Indian — a more uncomfortable truth than blaming Silicon Valley, but a more useful one. And it is not a permanent feature of the landscape. It is the consequence of decisions, which means it can be changed by decisions. But you cannot change what you have not measured, and India has not, until now, measured this.

CHAPTER FIVE

The Invoice That Was Never Sent

There is a question that Suman has never been asked and that no Indian government institution has ever formally posed: *what is the value of what you gave away today?*

Not the value of what he received. That is calculable, more or less. The answer about wheat streak mosaic virus was worth eight per cent of a yield. These are real values and they can, with effort, be estimated.

The question is about the other direction. The query Suman typed, the photograph he submitted, the agricultural vocabulary he reached for, the gap between what he could see and what he could name — what was that worth to the system that received it?

The answer is: we do not know. And the reason we do not know is not that the question is unanswerable. It is that no one with the authority to demand an answer has asked it. The invoice for this transfer was never sent. The line item was never entered. The category does not exist in any balance sheet India publishes — which means a transfer of potentially enormous value, recurring and compounding and accelerating, is happening in complete institutional silence. This chapter is about that silence.

To understand what data is worth, you have to understand what it is *for*. Data, in the form technology companies collect it, is not valuable in isolation. A single query from Suman about yellowing wheat is worth almost nothing by itself. What makes it valuable is accumulation. A million queries from a million Indian farmers about a million crop problems, in a dozen Indian languages, with attached photographs, gathered over years — that becomes something categorically different from any individual query. It becomes a training dataset, and the training dataset becomes a product, and the product becomes the thing that everyone in the market has to pay to use.

This dataset does not exist anywhere in the world in the form that Suman and farmers like him are currently building it. The agricultural knowledge embedded in Indian farming — accumulated across millennia of cultivation in the specific soils and climates of the subcontinent, encoded in the specific languages and dialects of the regions where it developed — has never been systematically collected in machine-readable form. It existed only in the hands and memories of a hundred and fifty million households. The smartphone is the collection mechanism. Every query is a deposit into a vault that Indians are filling and someone else holds the keys to.

Agriculture is one example. The most valuable data India generates is behavioural. When Priya paused on the kajal reel, that pause was recorded — the precise duration of her attention, the time of day, what she had seen immediately before, what she moved to immediately after — and added to a profile that has been accumulating since she first installed the app. What is less often discussed is *why Indian behavioural data is worth more than most.* Two reasons. The first is scale: five hundred million active users, generating data continuously across a range of contexts no research design could replicate. The second is diversity: India is not one population but a continent — twenty-two scheduled languages, hundreds of dialects, every income band and life circumstance present at once. A system trained on Indian data is more robust, more generalizable, and more valuable across the full range of human experience than a system trained anywhere else. India is not merely a large training set. It is the best one.

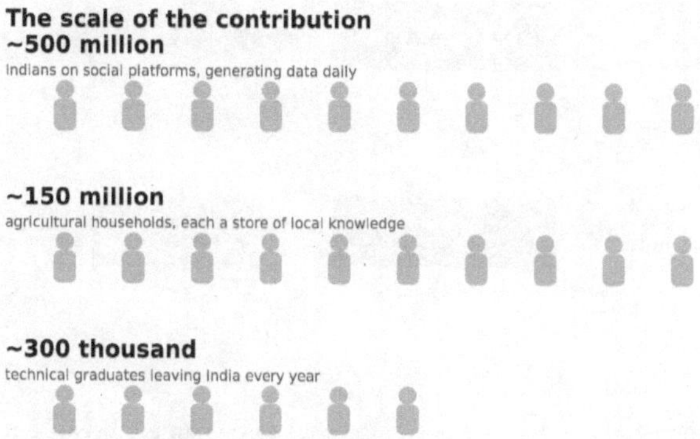

Figure 3. Each icon is illustrative, not to exact scale. Sources: industry estimates; Agriculture Census.

Here is where the silence becomes consequential.

The AI systems being built right now, on training data that includes Suman's crop queries and Priya's scroll behaviour and the purchase patterns of four hundred million Indian shoppers, will be deployed. They will be the interface through which Indian farmers get crop advice, Indian doctors get diagnostic support, Indian students learn. And the business model for the next generation of AI products is the access fee. The value of the training data is converted into a product; the product is sold to the people who need it; and in India's case there is a reasonable probability that many of those people will be the same communities whose data built it. The price for access has not yet been set. It will be higher than zero.

There is a name for this structure in economics. When someone takes a raw material, processes it, and sells the processed product back to the people who supplied the raw material — at a price that exceeds what they were paid for the raw material, which here was nothing — it is called a value-added processing model. The cotton is grown in one place, spun and woven somewhere else, and sold back as cloth at a margin. India has seen this exact model before, and not as a metaphor. For two centuries, Indian raw cotton was shipped to mills in Lancashire and returned as finished textile, and the difference between the price of the boll and the price of the bolt was the engine of someone else's industrial revolution. The data economy has rebuilt the arrangement in software. The raw material this time is not cotton. It is cognition.

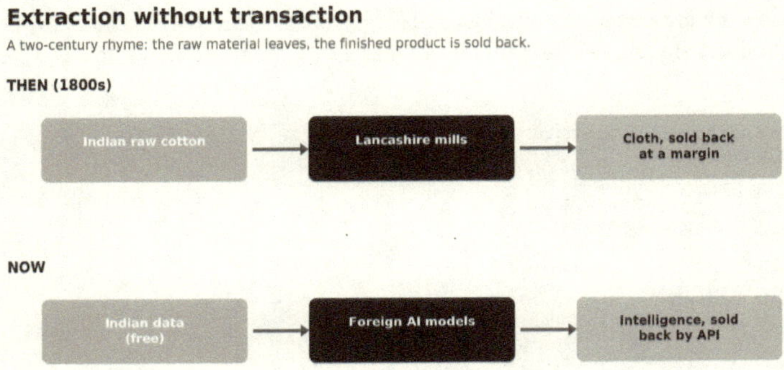

Figure 5. The value-added processing model, rebuilt in software. (Chapter 5)

There is one more dimension to Category Seven that has to be named, because it is the one that makes delay so expensive: *longitudinal depth.* The most capable AI systems are built on the most comprehensive datasets, and the most comprehensive datasets include the deepest records over time. Meta has been collecting Indian behavioural data since roughly 2010. Google has been collecting Indian search data since roughly 2005. Fifteen and twenty years of continuous observation across hundreds of millions of people is an asset that cannot be reconstructed by starting today — you cannot buy back the past. India cannot recover the data that has already been generated and transferred. That is gone. What India *can* do is decide, starting now, what happens to the twenty years of data that will be generated next.

India currently has no systematic mechanism for measuring data flows of this kind. The Digital Personal Data Protection Act of 2023 establishes principles for handling personal data — consent for collection, obligations for processors — and it is a meaningful step. But it is primarily a framework for protecting individual privacy, which is a different problem from accounting for the collective economic value of data generated by Indian users. The current framework thinks of data as a privacy issue. The framework that does not yet exist thinks of data as an economic resource — something whose value should be measured, accounted for, and potentially retained.

India needs its own accounting. Not because the companies collecting the data are acting illegally, but because you cannot make decisions about something you have not measured. The first invoice that was never sent needs to be sent. Every year it remains unsent is a year in which the transfer continues unremarked, uncontested, and compounding. The trajectory that this produces is the subject of the next chapter — because the transfer described in Chapters Four and Five is not merely large. It is built, by the logic of the system itself, to perpetuate itself.

CHAPTER SIX

The Trap That Sets Itself

Arjun did not choose dependency.

He chose AWS. That choice, made on a Tuesday in 2019 in eleven minutes, was sensible given everything available to him at the time. It was a choice for productivity, for speed, for tools that worked. It was not a choice for dependency. The dependency came later, the way most structural conditions arrive: not as a single event but as an accumulation of individually reasonable decisions whose collective effect only becomes visible from a distance.

This is the chapter about that mechanism — about why the transfer of the previous two chapters cannot be solved by individual decision-makers making better individual choices. Arjun cannot simply migrate. Priya cannot simply switch platforms. Suman cannot simply use a different search engine. Not because they lack the will, but because the structure they are inside was built — not intentionally, but effectively — to make those individual decisions harder with every passing month.

The name for the structure is lock-in. The mechanism is compounding switching costs. And the reason it perpetuates itself is that the same logic that makes it rational for Arjun to stay on AWS makes it rational for the *next* Arjun, founding his company next year, to begin on AWS. The trap is not a prison with walls. It is an equilibrium — which is far harder to escape, because no one is holding the door shut.

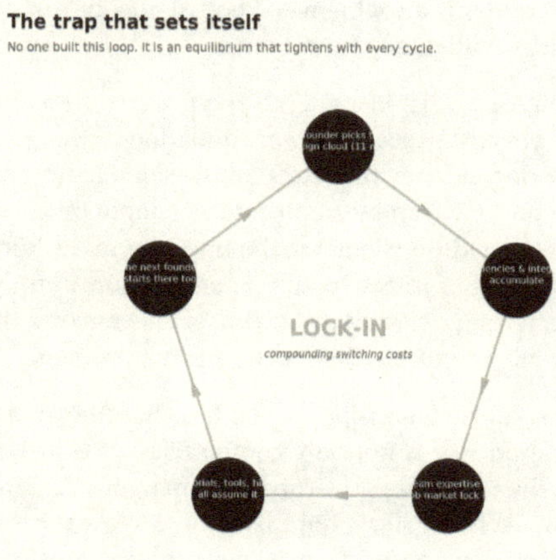

Figure 4. The dependency is structural, not a bad decision by any individual. (Chapter 6)

A switching cost is anything that makes it more expensive to leave a system than to stay. Lakshmi's seventy-to-ninety-lakh migration estimate is an *explicit* switching cost: it can be calculated, it appears in a spreadsheet, and it leads to a clear decision — do not migrate. But explicit switching costs are only the visible surface. Beneath them lie *implicit* switching costs, which are harder to measure, easier to ignore, and typically much larger.

The first is technical debt in the form of dependencies. Every managed service Arjun's platform uses, every integration with another AWS-native service, is a dependency, and dependencies compound. The platform that had twenty in 2019 has eighty in 2024 — not because anyone planned it, but because when you are building fast and a managed service exists that solves your problem, you use it.

The second is knowledge capital. Lakshmi knows AWS. Her team knows AWS. The job postings she writes assume AWS experience. A migration does not just rebuild the architecture; it rebuilds the team's expertise, and expertise is slow and expensive to rebuild.

The third is sector gravity. The tools developers in Bangalore use are, in the vast majority, built to work with AWS. The tutorials assume it. The conferences teach it. An alternative provider does not merely have to be technically competitive; it has to compete against a gravitational field created by the accumulated choices of millions of developers. None of this was created by a plan. It is the emergent property of a network effect operating over time.

And lock-in is not only a founder's problem. Priya is locked into Instagram not by any contract but because her cousins are there, her school parents' group is there, and fifteen years of photographs and connections that exist nowhere else are there. Her switching cost is not technical; it is social and emotional, and it is no less binding for that — arguably more, because you can hire engineers to rebuild a database but you cannot hire anyone to rebuild fifteen years of your family being in one place. Suman is locked into Google not because there is no other search engine but because Google, trained on more queries from more users over more years, simply gives better answers; any alternative he tried today would be worse, because it has not had twenty years of his community's questions to learn from. His switching cost is *quality* — the cruelest kind, because the incumbent earns it fairly and keeps it structurally.

At the level of individual decisions, none of this is problematic. It is simply how systems that produce value also capture it. At the level of national economic structure, the aggregate of these rational individual trades is a problem — because the lock-in does not just bind current users. It shapes the choices available to future ones.

Economists have a name for a related pattern: the poverty trap, a self-reinforcing cycle in which the conditions of poverty prevent the accumulation of the resources needed to escape poverty. The technology-dependency trap runs on the same logic, and it has the same escape route. You do not exit a poverty trap by lecturing the people inside it to make better choices. You exit it by changing the conditions outside the trap. Arjun deciding to migrate would cost his company one to two years of infrastructure spending for an uncertain saving and a real risk. He is not making a wrong decision by staying. He is making the only rational decision available inside the current structure. The structure is the problem.

And the structure has one more dimension the analysis has not yet named. The lock-in Arjun and Priya and Suman experience is not only commercial. It is jurisdictional. When Arjun's platform runs on AWS, the terms are governed by Amazon's customer agreement, which is subject to American law. When Priya's data lives on Meta's servers, the terms are subject to American law and, in relevant respects, to American government authority. This will not matter on most days. It will matter on a specific day — when an American regulator restricts the export of a technology India depends on, or an American court orders the disclosure of data held on behalf of Indian users. The trap sets itself economically, through switching costs. It reinforces itself jurisdictionally, through terms of service no one reads. And it compresses itself temporally: every year without alternatives is a year in which the switching cost grows, the jurisdictional exposure deepens, and the window for independent action narrows.

The coffee is cold; Arjun forgot it when the Hamburg call ran long. He makes a fresh cup. Twelve employees, a product that works, an AWS bill that arrives on the third of each month and is paid on the fifth, automatically, by a card that charges in rupees and settles in dollars. He does not think about this. There is no reason for him to. The reason to think about it does not live at the level of his individual decisions. It lives at the level of the structure that makes his decisions inevitable — and structures, unlike individual choices, can be changed.

CHAPTER SEVEN

Whose Law Governs Your Data

On the fourteenth of August — Pakistan's Independence Day and the eve of India's — a scenario no one has publicly planned for becomes a scenario worth planning for.

Imagine — and this is a constructed scenario, not a prediction — that a serious military incident occurs along the Line of Control. Not a war, but an escalation severe enough that the United States, balancing its relationships in the region, issues a partial sanctions designation affecting certain categories of financial and technology transfers connected to the affected zone. The designation is precise in its legal language and imprecise in its practical application, the way such designations often are. The legal teams at Amazon, Microsoft, and Google receive it on a Friday afternoon, Washington time. By Monday morning, their interpretation is that a temporary suspension of services to some categories of Indian customers is required while the scope is clarified. The suspension flags three thousand Indian companies for manual review. For seventy-two hours, they cannot reach their cloud resources.

For Arjun, seventy-two hours without AWS is not an inconvenience. It is an extinction event.

This scenario has not happened. There is no current sanctions designation of this kind, and it is constructed to illustrate a risk, not to forecast an event. But the risk it illustrates is structural and real, and it does not depend on the scenario. It depends on two pieces of American law that already exist.

The first is the CLOUD Act — the Clarifying Lawful Overseas Use of Data Act, passed by the United States Congress in 2018. It establishes that American law enforcement can compel American technology companies to produce data stored on their servers *regardless of where in the world those servers are physically located.* India has not negotiated a bilateral agreement with the United States for reciprocal data access. As a practical matter, this means the data stored by Indian users and Indian companies on American cloud infrastructure is, in legal principle, accessible to American authorities through a valid court order — without any requirement that Indian authorities be notified or that Indian law apply. The mirage that server location confers sovereignty is exactly that: a mirage. The CLOUD Act exists precisely because, before it, the question of physical server location was litigated — in the *Microsoft Ireland* case, where the US government sought emails Microsoft stored in Dublin — and Congress resolved the ambiguity in favour of reach. Where the bytes sit is not where the jurisdiction sits.

The second is the Export Administration Regulations — the American rules governing the export of technology and technical data. A change in American foreign policy, a new sanctions designation, a new export-control determination, can alter the terms under which American cloud providers are legally permitted to serve Indian customers, with no input from India.

These are not hypothetical powers. They have been exercised. In 2018, ZTE — the Chinese telecommunications company — was cut off from American technology suppliers as part of a trade dispute. For several weeks it could not manufacture phones, because critical components came from American-controlled supply chains. The episode was alarming enough to Beijing that it accelerated a national program to build domestic alternatives across the semiconductor and software stack. The lesson China drew was not that the United States was hostile. It was that dependence is a vulnerability *whether or not* the other party is hostile, because the vulnerability is structural and the hostility is optional.

The point of this chapter is not that these powers will be exercised against India. The relationship between India and the United States is positive, multidimensional, and not currently characterized by the kind of tension that would make such exercise likely. The point is not the probability of the worst case. The point is the *consequence* of a dependency that makes the worst case possible. A nation whose critical digital infrastructure is governed by foreign law, stored on foreign servers, and subject to foreign regulatory authority has accepted a vulnerability that compounds over time. And the vulnerability is not contingent on the relationship turning adversarial. It is contingent on the relationship remaining *perfect* — not merely good today, but permanently good, under every future administration, across every future geopolitical development. History does not support that confidence.

There is a simpler version of the argument that needs no sanctions scenario at all. It needs only the CLOUD Act. Every Indian company that stores customer data on American cloud infrastructure has already accepted that the data is subject to American legal jurisdiction. The data of hundreds of millions of Indian citizens — their purchases, their medical searches, their financial transactions, their communications — sits in systems that are, in legal principle, reachable by a foreign government under foreign law. The protection is American, not Indian. It depends on American courts, American administrative practice, and the state of the bilateral relationship at any given moment. India does not have sovereignty over this data in the way the word *sovereignty* is normally understood.

A nation that cannot govern its own data cannot fully govern itself. This is not a proposition about technology. It is a proposition about sovereignty, which is what nations are for.

Priya's school is in a building that has stood since 1987. The desks are old, the ceiling fans are old, and it is imperfect in the specific ways underfunded public institutions in a developing country are imperfect. But it is hers, in the sense that matters: it is governed by Indian law, its teachers accountable to Indian parents and Indian boards and, ultimately, to the Indian state. The phone in her pocket is not. The difference between those two facts is what Part Two has been about. Now we need to look at what other nations did when they saw it clearly.

PART THREE

IT HAS BEEN DONE

What Others Built

The dependency described in Part Two can feel like weather — too large and too systemic to be the kind of thing a country decides about. Part Three exists to dissolve that feeling. Four nations looked at a version of the same problem and chose to act. None of them got everything right. None of their solutions can be lifted whole and dropped onto India. But together they prove the essential point: this is a problem that responds to decisions. China built walls. Europe wrote rules. South Korea built factories. Estonia built architecture. Each answer carries a lesson India can use and a mistake India must refuse. We take them one at a time, and then lay them side by side.

CHAPTER EIGHT

The Price of Walls

China solved the problem.

That sentence requires immediate qualification, because the way China solved it is not available to India, not compatible with India's constitutional structure, not desirable by India's own stated values, and not something this book recommends. The qualification matters. But the sentence also has to be said first, plainly, because the temptation in Indian discourse about China is to dismiss the comparison so quickly that the lesson gets dismissed along with it.

The mechanism is well known. Between roughly 1998 and 2010, China built or mandated domestic alternatives to every major foreign digital platform and then restricted access to the foreign originals. Google was effectively blocked in 2010, its market ceded to Baidu. Facebook was blocked in 2009, the space filled by what became WeChat and Weibo. YouTube was blocked and replaced by Youku and a proliferation of domestic video platforms. The domestic alternatives were not, in 2010, as good as the products they replaced. They were good enough, they were present, and the restriction of the foreign options meant Chinese developers, Chinese investors, and Chinese users had no choice but to make them better.

They made them better.

This is the part of the China story that is uncomfortable to acknowledge in any context where the political model is rightly criticized, but it is true and it matters. The platforms that emerged from the forced substitution of the 2000s are, in 2026, exceptional by any technical standard. WeChat is a more sophisticated product than WhatsApp. Alibaba's cloud competes with AWS across Asia on capability and price. TikTok is the most successful Chinese digital export in history, built on recommendation infrastructure refined first in the protected domestic market and then turned outward against the very companies that were once kept out. Protection, in the Chinese case, was not the opposite of excellence. It was the nursery for it.

The cost was real, and it has to be stated with equal plainness. Chinese internet users cannot reach Google, or Wikipedia in its standard form, or news sources the state deems inconvenient. The Great Firewall is not only an instrument of technological independence; it is also an instrument of political control, and the two functions cannot be cleanly separated. This is the reason the Chinese model is unavailable to India — not primarily because of technical complexity, but because India is a democracy, with a free press, with constitutional protections for expression, and a civil society that would correctly treat the construction of a Great Firewall as an assault on its founding values. The Chinese model requires a degree of state authority over information flows that the Indian constitutional order forbids. That is not a limitation to be regretted. It is a feature of the system India chose. But it means the Chinese path is one India cannot walk.

What India *can* take from China is narrower and more specific than the overall model, but it is not nothing.

The first lesson is about *sequencing*. China did not wait for its domestic platforms to become competitive before restricting the foreign ones. It restricted first and invested in competitiveness second. India cannot and must not replicate that sequencing through restriction. But it can replicate the underlying move — guaranteeing a domestic market before the product is world-beating — through *procurement* rather than prohibition. The Indian government is one of the largest technology buyers on earth. A policy that directs a meaningful share of that procurement toward domestic alternatives creates a captive market large enough to fund the development of products that can eventually win on merit. This is not radical. It is standard industrial policy, practised by every nation that has ever built a technology sector. Government as first customer is the oldest technology-development strategy in the world.

The second lesson is about *data*. China's domestic platforms accumulated Chinese behavioural data that foreign AI developers never obtained. India's data did not stay behind any wall; it has been accumulating in foreign systems for two decades, and that history cannot be undone. But the data generated over the *next* two decades is not yet allocated, and the Chinese experience demonstrates the value of keeping it close.

The third lesson is the most uncomfortable, and it requires precision to avoid being misread. China proved that the network-effect problem — the gravitational pull of established foreign platforms — *can be broken* by a sufficiently determined intervention. The pull of Google and Facebook was real in China in 2009; the state broke it by removing the option of staying. India should not do this. But India should absorb the underlying fact: network effects, however powerful, are not laws of physics. They can be disrupted. The disruption requires something the market alone will not supply. It does not, however, require walls.

China saw the dependency as an economic problem before it was anything else — the recognition that a country running its digital economy on foreign infrastructure is permanently subordinate, and that technology dependence is a structural extraction that compound interest will worsen over time. That *framing* is available to India, and it is arguably the more powerful one for India's purposes. Security arguments can be waved away as paranoia. Economic arguments, especially at the magnitude of Chapter Four, are far harder to dismiss. The thirty-billion-dollar architecture is not a threat. It is a price. China decided the price was too high and paid for independence in a currency — political freedom — that India should not and need not spend. The question for India is whether a different intervention, one that needs no walls, can reach a comparable result. The European Union tried to answer that question through regulation rather than construction. The results are instructive.

CHAPTER NINE

Regulation Without Construction

The European Union has spent more than fifteen years trying to solve a version of India's problem through law.

The tools it built are genuinely impressive. The General Data Protection Regulation, in force since 2018, is the most comprehensive data-protection framework in the world: it establishes rights for European citizens over their personal data, imposes obligations on the companies that collect it, requires explicit consent for most uses, and authorizes fines of up to four per cent of global annual revenue. It has been enforced with teeth — Meta alone has been fined well over a billion euros across multiple decisions, Google several times more. The Digital Markets Act, in force since 2023, goes further still, designating the largest companies as "gatekeepers" and imposing specific obligations: interoperability with competitors, prohibitions on using business users' data to compete against them, the right for users to uninstall pre-loaded apps.

And yet.

Europe does not have a global technology company. It has no cloud provider competing with AWS, Azure, or Google Cloud at global scale. It has no social-media platform of consequence, no search engine of consequence. GAIA-X, the European cloud initiative launched with fanfare at a Franco-German summit in October 2020, was meant to create a trusted European data infrastructure; years later it exists primarily as a standards body — working groups and specification documents and very little operational infrastructure. The major cloud services European companies actually use remain American. The fines flow into the EU budget. The data continues to flow to California.

This is not a criticism of the European project so much as a diagnosis of its limits. The GDPR has genuinely changed how technology companies handle personal data worldwide, not only in Europe; the Digital Markets Act is reshaping platform behaviour in ways that benefit users everywhere. But enforcement against existing infrastructure is not the same as building alternative infrastructure. Regulation can constrain how foreign companies behave in your market. It cannot, by itself, conjure the domestic capability that would let your market operate independently. A fine on Meta does not create a European social network. A competition ruling against Google does not create a European search engine.

The structural reason for the gap is worth naming, because India will hit the same wall if it tries to follow the European path. Regulation is, by design, *backward-looking*. It responds to what existing companies have already done. That is entirely appropriate for law and entirely mismatched to the problem of building alternatives, which requires *forward-looking* investment in things that do not yet exist. GAIA-X is the clearest illustration of the chasm between regulatory ambition and infrastructure reality: announced as a European cloud, delivered as a committee. American companies, subject to American law, still process European data under American terms of service.

The lesson for India is not that regulation is useless. It is that regulation *alone* is insufficient. India needs regulation of the kind Europe pioneered — the DPDP Act is a beginning — but regulation has to be paired with construction. The relationship between the two is precise and worth stating as a rule: *if you have no alternative to AWS, regulating AWS is the only move available, and it is a weak one. If you have a credible alternative to AWS, regulation becomes powerful, because it can accelerate migration toward the alternative rather than merely policing behaviour inside the dependency.* Regulation without construction constrains the tenant. Regulation with construction lets the tenant become an owner.

There is one specific European instrument India should study closely. The European Data Act, in force since 2024, creates rights for users and businesses to access and share the data generated by their use of connected products and services. It is an attempt to build a framework in which the *economic* value of data — not merely its privacy — is governed by rules that prevent its unilateral capture by platform operators. This is far closer to the Category Seven problem than anything in the GDPR. It reflects a recognition, in European law, that the data problem is not only a privacy problem; it is a property problem. *Who owns the data a person generates through their behaviour?* is a question Indian law has not yet answered in any systematic way. It needs an answer. Europe is developing one. India should develop its own, fitted to India's situation rather than imported wholesale.

Europe regulated. It produced the best regulatory framework in the world, and it is not enough. What Europe needed alongside the rules is what South Korea actually built. Europe defined the rules of the road better than anyone and is still driving on someone else's road. India should watch this carefully — and build the road.

CHAPTER TEN

The Samsung Lesson

In 1969, the Korean government decided it would build a semiconductor industry.

Korea did not have one. It did not have the engineering talent, the capital, the technology, or the manufacturing base to build one. What it had was a government that had studied what Japan did in the previous two decades and decided Korea would do the same. The decision was not made by the market. The market, in 1969, would never have invested in Korean semiconductors: the risk was too high, the capability gap too wide, the competition too entrenched. A rational investor looking at Korean semiconductor capacity in 1969 would have concluded the opportunity cost made no sense.

The government invested anyway — not blindly. The strategy was carefully built: targets chosen with reference to where the technology was heading rather than where it stood, the investment paired with aggressive expansion of engineering education. But it was unambiguously a strategic decision made *outside* the logic of contemporary market returns, in anticipation of a competitive position that did not yet exist.

What followed is the most successful technology industrialization story of the twentieth century. By the 1980s, Korean firms — Samsung, LG, what became SK Hynix — were producing chips that competed with Japanese and American products on quality. By the 1990s they led in memory. By the 2000s Samsung was the largest semiconductor company in the world by revenue. Today South Korea produces roughly a fifth of global semiconductor output, and a single Korean company sits at the centre of the most strategically contested supply chain on earth.

This is the Samsung lesson, and it is not about Samsung.

The lesson is about the relationship between strategic intent, patient capital, and time. The semiconductor investment did not pay back on a five-year horizon, or a ten-year horizon. The payback period was closer to twenty years — longer than any electoral cycle, longer than any private fund's holding period. The reason it happened anyway is that the Korean state chose to treat industrial capacity in strategic sectors as a *national interest* rather than a market opportunity. A national interest can accept a longer horizon, because the return it seeks — strategic autonomy, economic independence, the capacity to compete — is not denominated in the currency of quarterly earnings.

India has done exactly this before. In nuclear technology, India built domestic capability against active technology-denial regimes and international sanctions. In space, ISRO built launch vehicles and satellites at a fraction of the cost of foreign alternatives, through patient public investment in engineering capability that took decades to mature. The precedent for strategic investment in *capability* over market-determined investment in *returns* is not foreign to India. It is written through India's own post-independence history.

Part of the reason this logic has not been applied to digital infrastructure is a category error. Cloud platforms, social networks, and software services look, from a certain angle, like ordinary commercial products that the market should provide — and usually the market should.

But digital infrastructure of the foundational kind is, in economic terms, closer to a *public good*: something whose value to any one user rises with how widely it is used, and whose total social value therefore exceeds what any individual user or private investor would pay for it. Roads are public goods. Power grids are public goods. So, it turns out, are payment rails — which is why the clearest proof of the argument is one India already possesses. UPI is a public digital good, built through the National Payments Corporation of India with public backing, opened to private operators on equal terms, and now processing well over a hundred and eighty billion transactions a year. It is the most successful real-time payments infrastructure in the world, and it would not exist if the decision had been left to the private market on commercial terms.

The Samsung lesson is not that the government should build the national champion. Korea did not have the state build Samsung. The lesson is that the state created the *conditions* — the capital, the protected early market, the talent pipeline, the time — within which a private company could grow to global scale. The government did not produce the chips. It produced the environment in which the company that produced the chips could exist. South Korea built the conditions; the market built the company; both were necessary, and neither alone would have sufficed.

There is a timing dimension India cannot afford to ignore. Korea began in 1969, and by the time Korean chips were competitive the window to establish a dominant position was still open. India has perhaps a five-to-ten-year window in which patient investment in domestic AI and cloud infrastructure can still produce systems competitive at meaningful scale. After that window, the switching costs and capability gaps will have compounded to the point where catching up requires not just investment but fundamental breakthroughs that cannot be scheduled. The Samsung lesson is as much about timing as about strategy. Korea's window was open for decades. India's is open for years.

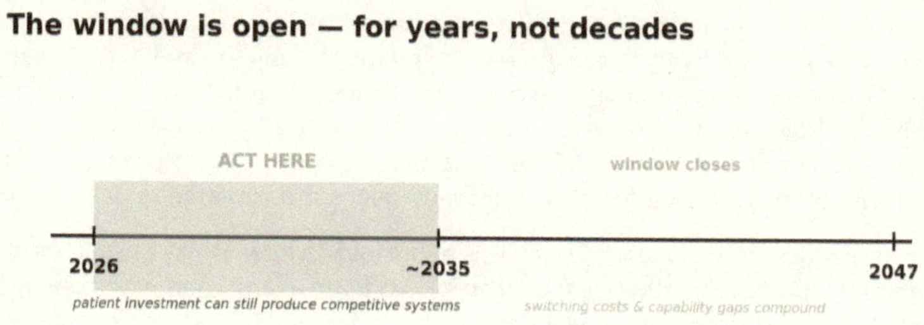

Figure 9. The Samsung lesson is as much about timing as strategy. (Chapters 10 & 17)

CHAPTER ELEVEN

One Million People Proved It

Estonia has a population of roughly 1.4 million people.

It is smaller than Bengaluru. It is smaller than Ahmedabad. It is smaller than Surat. By the measures that usually determine national capacity, it has no business appearing on any list of nations India should study for lessons about building digital infrastructure at scale. It appears on this list for a different reason: not for what its size makes possible, but for what its thinking made possible.

In 1991, when Estonia regained independence from the Soviet Union, it inherited a Soviet bureaucracy, Soviet physical infrastructure, and essentially no functioning digital infrastructure of any kind. It faced a choice: build the digital layer of its new state on foreign systems, or build it from scratch as domestic public infrastructure. It built from scratch. The reason was partly philosophical and partly brutally practical — Estonia was too small to be a priority market for the major foreign platforms, and localizing their services for a language spoken by about a million people was not commercially attractive. If Estonia wanted digital services, it had to build them itself.

So it did. The X-Road system, launched in 2001, is a distributed data-exchange layer that lets different government and private databases communicate securely *without* centralizing data in any single repository. Every Estonian has a cryptographically secured digital identity that can be used to access any government service, sign any legal document, vote in national elections, read medical records, and transact with any private institution connected to the system. The results are quantifiable: Estonia delivers ninety-nine per cent of government services digitally, tax returns are filed in minutes, and a company can be incorporated in under an hour.

The Estonian lesson is not about size. It is about *architecture*. What Estonia built keeps data distributed rather than centralized; uses open standards so any compliant system can connect; makes the public infrastructure available to private actors on equal terms; and keeps the identity and authentication layer in public hands. This is the exact opposite of the architecture that produced the thirty-billion-dollar dependency. The dependency is built on centralized platforms, each company holding its users' data in a proprietary silo that others can reach only by paying for access on commercial terms. The Estonian architecture leaves data with its owners and provides a neutral public rail through which it can be shared — on the owner's terms, when the owner chooses.

India has built pieces of exactly this. Aadhaar is the largest biometric identity system in the world, providing a digital identity to roughly 1.38 billion people. DigiLocker gives citizens digital access to official documents. The Account Aggregator framework lets citizens share financial data with institutions they choose, on consent terms they control. These are not small achievements; taken together with UPI and ONDC, they represent the most significant deployment of digital public goods outside China in the history of the internet. The question is why the same architectural logic has not been extended to the rest of the stack.

Estonia's infrastructure has one property India's does not yet fully share: it covers the *entire* stack. X-Road connects not only government services but private-sector services; the digital identity is used not just for voting and tax but for every commercial transaction that requires authentication. The infrastructure is not a government service running parallel to the private sector. It is the substrate on which both operate. India's digital public goods do this in specific domains — UPI is the substrate for payments, Aadhaar increasingly for identity verification — but the cloud most Indian companies run on is not Indian public infrastructure, the data layer is not Indian public infrastructure, and the AI layer being built on top of that data is not Indian public infrastructure. The gap between what India has built and what Estonia has built is not a gap of ambition or capability. It is a gap of *scope*. India applied the public-infrastructure logic to the transaction layer and stopped. Estonia applied it to the whole stack, including the data layer.

The lesson is not to copy Estonia's specific systems — a nation of 1.4 billion cannot simply scale up what a nation of 1.4 million built. The lesson is to apply the same *principle* — public infrastructure for the foundational layer, private competition for the services built on top — to the parts of the stack India has not yet covered.

Estonia also learned something India should absorb before, not after, it is forced to. When Russia demonstrated, in 2007, that it was willing to conduct cyberattacks against Estonian infrastructure, Estonia had to confront a question it had treated as theoretical: what happens to a nation whose entire government runs on digital infrastructure when that infrastructure is attacked? The answer was not to reduce digital dependence but to build resilience and *jurisdiction* into it. Estonia established "data embassies" — servers located in friendly foreign countries but legally treated as Estonian territory, governed by Estonian law — and engineered X-Road to be distributed enough that no single point of failure could bring it down. Estonia built jurisdiction into the architecture. India is building digital infrastructure at extraordinary scale, and jurisdiction is not yet fully built in. Building it in is far easier before the infrastructure is complete than after.

Priya. Arjun. Suman. Three people whose choices built a structure they did not choose. China built walls. Europe wrote rules. South Korea built factories. Estonia built architecture. Each solved a version of the problem. None solved it in a way India can simply adopt. Lay them on a single table and the pattern becomes a strategy:

Nation	Instrument	What it got right	What India cannot / must not copy	The transferable lesson
China	Walls + forced substitution	Broke the network effect; built world-class platforms; framed dependency as economic	Censorship; state control of information	Guarantee a domestic market — but through **procurement, not prohibition**
European Union	Regulation (GDPR, DMA, Data Act)	Best rules in the world; reframed data as property	Regulating without building — constraining the tenant, never becoming the owner	Pair regulation **with construction;** study the Data Act's economic-value model

Nation	Instrument	What it got right	What India cannot / must not copy	The transferable lesson
South Korea	Industrial policy + patient capital	Treated capability as national interest; 20-year horizon; conditions for a private champion	Nothing to refuse — India has done this in nuclear, space, UPI	Public **conditions,** private company; act inside the open window
Estonia	Open, distributed public architecture	Whole-stack public infrastructure; jurisdiction built into the design	Its small scale	Extend India's DPI logic to the **whole stack,** jurisdiction included

Four answers, one axis

Built vs. regulated × walled vs. open. India can aim for the corner none of them reached.

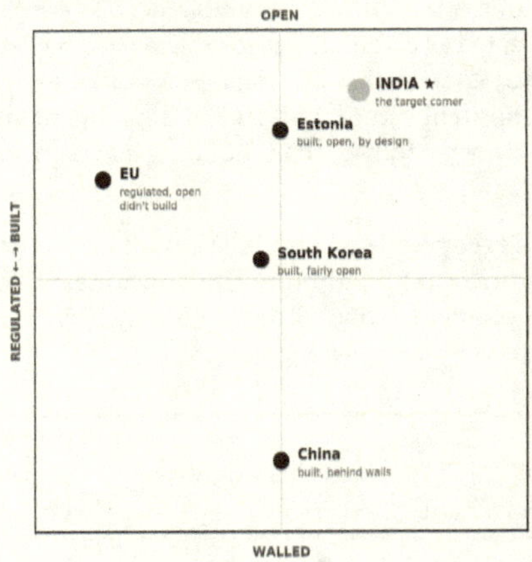

Figure 6. Synthesis of Part Three. Positions are illustrative.

What India has that none of them had is the subject of the next part.

PART FOUR

WHAT INDIA HAS

Advantages Nobody Is Counting

Every chapter so far has been, in one way or another, about a cost. Part Four is about an inventory. Before India can decide whether to build an alternative, it has to take an honest measure of what it already owns — and the honest measure is startling, because India has quietly built more of the answer than almost anyone, inside India or outside it, has registered. It has built payment rails the world is now copying. It produces the engineering talent that runs the rival's industry. And it holds a diplomatic position that, in the current technological moment, is worth more than either. These are assets nobody is counting. This part counts them.

CHAPTER TWELVE

The Stack That Already Works

In 2009, sending money from a bank account in Mumbai to a bank account in Chennai took three business days.

This was not a failure of Indian banking. It was the state of banking everywhere. The infrastructure for moving money between institutions was built in an era of paper and batch processing, and it moved at the speed of paper and batch processing even after the paper became digital. The United States still has this problem; a domestic wire transfer initiated at an American bank counter can take one to three business days to settle.

India solved it. Not partially, not for some transactions, not in a pilot that works only for the technically sophisticated. India solved it completely, at population scale, for every citizen with a phone number.

UPI — the Unified Payments Interface — processed on the order of one hundred and eighty-five billion transactions in the fiscal year ending March 2025, and the run-rate has only climbed since. That figure is larger than the combined transaction volume of Visa and Mastercard globally, measured by count rather than value. The average transaction settles in under three seconds. The system runs twenty-four hours a day, every day of the year, including holidays. It is free for users. It works on a four-thousand-rupee phone over a patchy 4G connection. It is, by a wide margin, the most significant financial-infrastructure innovation of the twenty-first century — and it happened in India, built by Indian engineers, funded by Indian public investment, deployed at a scale no other nation has matched.

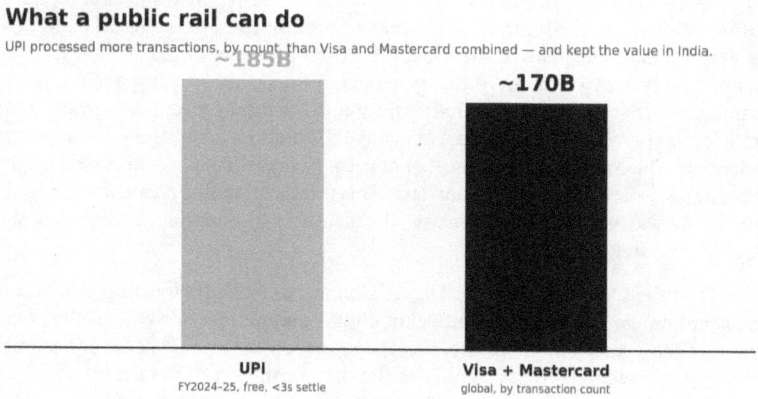

Figure 8. Transaction count, not value. Sources: NPCI; network disclosures. (Chapter 12)

UPI did not happen because the Indian private sector decided to build it. The private sector was building what the private sector builds: products that capture value for the companies that make them. UPI happened because the National Payments Corporation of India — a public institution created under the aegis of the Reserve Bank — decided to build a public good. The NPCI built the rails. Private companies built the trains that run on them: PhonePe, Google Pay, Paytm, and dozens of others compete fiercely on the user experience. But because the rails are public and access is equal, no single private company can lock users in, levy a private toll on every transaction, or accumulate a proprietary monopoly over the payment graph. The result is a payments system that serves users rather than platforms. And the consequence of a payments system that serves users rather than platforms is that India's domestic payments simply do not appear in the Category One-through-Six accounting of Chapter Four. One hundred and eighty-five billion transactions a year, and not a dollar of the value they represent leaks out of the country. This is what public digital infrastructure looks like when it works — and it is the single most important fact in this book, because it is the existence proof. India did not theorize this. India shipped it.

Aadhaar is the second piece. The biometric identity system India built between 2009 and 2016 is, by any measure, the largest identity-infrastructure project in human history, enrolling roughly 1.38 billion people. It gives a verifiable digital identity to citizens who previously had no reliable document-based identity at all — the migrant worker, the rural woman without a birth certificate, the informal-economy participant invisible to every formal system. The criticisms are real and should be named: the original architecture concentrated too much data in a central database; the mandatory-linkage debates raised legitimate constitutional questions about consent and exclusion; the Supreme Court's 2018 judgment rightly constrained some of the more aggressive proposals. These criticisms have improved the system and should continue to be taken seriously. But a billion and a half people with verifiable digital identities is an infrastructure asset of extraordinary value — the authentication layer on which every other digital service can be built. It is the reason Direct Benefit Transfers have moved enormous sums directly to citizens with a documented reduction in leakage that the government estimates in the lakhs of crores.

The Account Aggregator framework is the third piece, and the least known of the three. Operational since 2021, it lets Indian citizens share their financial data with institutions of their choosing, on consent terms they control, through an architecture that is deliberately neutral. The citizen does not share data *with* the Account Aggregator. The Account Aggregator is a consent manager — a licensed entity that facilitates the secure transfer of data from the institution holding it to the institution the citizen has authorized to receive it, without itself storing or reading the data. This is the Category Seven problem solved architecturally, in one domain. The financial data an Indian generates through her banking behaviour is, under this framework, *hers*: the institution that wants it must request consent, she grants or denies it, the transfer happens, and she remains in control throughout. And the same architecture can be extended. The consent framework that governs financial data can, in principle, govern health data, agricultural data, educational data. This is not a plan that needs inventing. The architecture exists, the regulatory model exists, the institutional precedent exists. What it needs is the decision to extend it.

ONDC — the Open Network for Digital Commerce — is the fourth piece, and perhaps the most ambitious. The dominant model of digital commerce worldwide is the platform model: one company runs a marketplace, sets the terms for buyers and sellers, takes a commission on every transaction, and accumulates the data from every interaction. ONDC proposes a different architecture. Instead of a single platform, it is a network protocol — a standard that lets any buyer-facing app talk to any seller-facing app without either having to live on the same platform. It applies the UPI principle to commerce: make the rail public and open, and let private players compete on the experience above it. It is early, and unproven at full scale, but the architecture is right, and "the architecture is right" is the hardest thing to get and the easiest to extend.

Taken together — UPI, Aadhaar, the Account Aggregator framework, ONDC, DigiLocker, and the emerging digital health stack — India has built something no other nation at its economic level possesses: a substantial layer of digital public infrastructure that operates *outside* the dependency architecture of Part Two. This stack is not complete. It does not cover cloud infrastructure, where the dependency is most acute. It does not cover the AI layer. It does not cover search or social. But it is far more than most people know, and it is the foundation on which the missing pieces can be built.

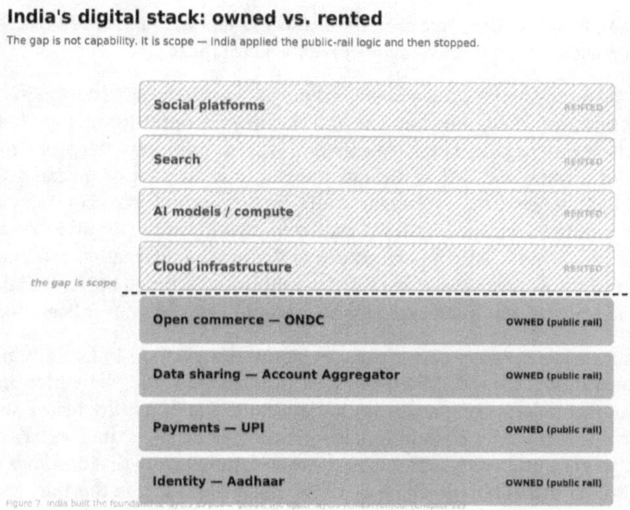

Figure 7. India built the found

The argument that India cannot build its own technology infrastructure has already been answered — India built UPI, and the argument is over. The question now is not *whether* India can build. It is *what* remains to be built, how fast, and with what resources.

CHAPTER THIRTEEN

India's Most Expensive Export

Every year, roughly three hundred thousand Indians with advanced degrees in engineering, computer science, and related technical fields leave India.

They go primarily to the United States, where they form the largest foreign-born population in the American technology sector. They go because the opportunities are better — the salaries higher, the infrastructure better, the companies more ambitious, the problems more interesting. This is not a conspiracy. It is the rational response to a set of incentives India has not yet managed to change. The engineer from IIT Bombay who joins a company in Mountain View is not betraying India; she is making the same kind of rational individual choice Arjun made when he chose AWS. The opportunity was there. The alternative was not better enough to choose. But the aggregate of three hundred thousand rational individual decisions to leave is an annual transfer of human capital whose cost to India has never been formally calculated.

The American technology sector runs, in significant part, on Indian engineering talent. The chief executives of Google, Microsoft, IBM, Adobe, Palo Alto Networks, and dozens of other American technology companies are Indian-born. The founding teams and research labs of American AI companies contain Indians in numbers far exceeding India's share of the global population. The university labs where the foundational work that becomes next decade's technology is done are full of Indian researchers. India is producing this talent and exporting most of it.

The cost has two components. The first is direct and calculable. An undergraduate engineering degree at an IIT costs the Indian state roughly twenty to twenty-five lakh rupees per student in subsidized education. When that student graduates and moves abroad, the return on the Indian public's investment accrues to a foreign company and a foreign economy. The subsidy was Indian; the return is American. Across three hundred thousand departing technical graduates a year, the annual transfer of publicly funded human capital runs to the order of forty to fifty thousand crore rupees. Every year. It is, quite literally, one of India's largest exports — and the only major one for which India receives no payment.

The second component is harder to calculate and more consequential: the opportunity cost of the problems that go unsolved in India because the people who could solve them are solving different problems somewhere else. The AI systems that will govern Indian agriculture in 2035 are being built now, in significant part by Indians — in San Francisco and Seattle and London, on datasets that include Indian data, for companies that will sell the result back to India. The capability India needs to build its own AI layer is Indian. It is currently deployed elsewhere.

Why it is deployed elsewhere, and what it would take to deploy more of it at home, is the question Indian technology policy has been asking for twenty years without fully answering. The conventional answer is compensation: American companies pay more. This is true — a senior engineer in Mountain View earns, in dollar terms, three to five times what the most generous Indian employer pays, and even adjusted for cost of living the gap narrows but does not close. But compensation is not the whole answer, and the part it leaves out is the part that matters most for policy. The engineers who return to India are not, in the main, drawn back by a narrowing pay gap. They are drawn by the *quality of the problems.*

The most interesting problems in technology today are problems of scale and diversity. Building for a billion users who speak twenty-two languages, who reach the internet through a four-thousand-rupee phone on a 4G connection, who are making their first digital financial transaction, who are asking questions in agricultural vocabularies no system has ever been trained on — these are *harder* problems than building the next iteration of an American product for an American market that has been digitally saturated for two decades. India is the frontier. The engineers who understand this are coming back, or staying. Making that argument credibly — clearly, and backed by the infrastructure investment that makes it *true* rather than aspirational — is a large part of what would change the arithmetic.

The other part is giving them something to build on. An engineer who returns to work on agricultural AI needs data infrastructure to work with, compute that does not route her data and her models through foreign servers, a market that will adopt what she builds, and capital that will fund the time it takes. Some of this exists. Some is being built. Not enough of it exists fast enough.

But here is the fact the brain-drain conversation almost always misses, and it reframes the entire problem: *the capability does not need to be repatriated. It needs to be oriented.* An Indian engineer in San Francisco building an agricultural AI system for Indian farmers — funded by Indian public investment, trained on Indian data infrastructure, owned by an Indian institution — is doing something categorically different from the same engineer building advertising optimization for an American platform, even though neither of them has moved house. The diaspora is not a loss to be mourned and recovered. It is a distributed national asset that is currently pointed at someone else's problems. Consider a composite of the kind of person this describes: an engineer who left for a foreign AI lab in 2016, spent eight years at the frontier of large-model research, and in 2025 was offered the chance to lead the Indian-language model effort at a Bengaluru institute backed by public capital. She did not come back for the salary, which fell. She came back because the problem — teaching a machine what a farmer means by *yellowing at the stem* — was more interesting than anything on offer where she was, and because, for the first time, the infrastructure to attempt it existed at home. Multiply that decision by even a fraction of three hundred thousand and the arithmetic of the brain drain inverts. The talent was never the constraint. The orientation was.

The diaspora is not lost. It is unallocated.

CHAPTER FOURTEEN

Non-Alignment as a Product Feature

India has a foreign-policy posture it inherited from Nehru and has maintained, with varying consistency, through every government since: strategic autonomy. The refusal to be permanently aligned with any single bloc. The insistence on the right to independent judgment. The cultivation of relationships across the geopolitical spectrum that keeps India's options open.

This posture has been called many things — non-alignment in the Nehruvian era, strategic autonomy after the Cold War, multi-alignment in the current vocabulary. The label changes; the substance is constant: India will not be permanently subordinate to any external power's framework. For most of India's history this has been a diplomatic and military doctrine. What has not been fully recognized is that, in the current technological moment, the very same posture is an extraordinarily valuable *product feature.*

The world Priya and Arjun and Suman inhabit is one in which the two dominant technology spheres are American and Chinese. Nations that adopt the American sphere accept American legal jurisdiction over their data, American regulatory authority over their technology providers, and American foreign policy as the ultimate backstop of their infrastructure. Nations that adopt the Chinese sphere accept a different but symmetrical set of dependencies: Chinese technology companies are subject to Chinese law, including national-security provisions that compel cooperation with Chinese intelligence services. For many nations — particularly across the Global South — neither option is comfortable. The choice between them is a choice between two forms of dependency with different geopolitical strings attached.

India is one of the very few nations not required to make that choice. Its relationships with both powers are sufficiently developed, its independent capability sufficiently real, and its strategic position sufficiently important that it can credibly offer a third option: technology infrastructure that is neither American nor Chinese, built to Indian standards, governed by Indian law, and available to other nations on terms that do not require them to pick a side. This is not theoretical. It is precisely what Brazil, South Africa, Indonesia, Nigeria, Vietnam, and dozens of other nations are actively looking for — a technology partner that is not a great power, that does not arrive with the geopolitical strings that American or Chinese investment carries, and that has the scale and capability to actually build and maintain what they need. India is the only nation on earth that has, at once, the population scale, the engineering talent, the existing digital infrastructure, the diplomatic relationships, and the strategic autonomy to fill that role.

Non-alignment, for seventy-five years a diplomatic doctrine, is now a technology market position.

And the market is not waiting politely for India to notice. The nations of the Global South are building on whatever is available — primarily American platforms and Chinese infrastructure — because that is what is on offer. But the preference for a third option is explicit, and India has already proven it can be supplied. UPI is the demonstration. India has signed agreements to extend UPI's real-time payment rails internationally with a growing list of partners — among them Singapore, the United Arab Emirates, France, Mauritius, Sri Lanka, Nepal, and Bhutan.

The technical architecture is Indian. The regulatory model is Indian. The countries adopting it are choosing Indian infrastructure to run their own domestic and cross-border payments. This is not charity, and it is not soft power for its own sake. It is the early evidence of a market — the first proof that the world will choose an Indian rail when one is offered.

The same logic applies to every layer of the stack India builds at home. An identity infrastructure on the Aadhaar model, adapted to a partner country's legal and demographic conditions, is more attractive to many nations than a foreign-corporate alternative precisely because it arrives without the data-sovereignty concern that foreign ownership creates. A partner government in Africa or Southeast Asia weighing whose identity system to build its citizen services on is weighing, whether it says so or not, whose courts will ultimately reach that data. "Neither Washington nor Beijing" is, for that government, not a slogan but a specification.

India has the scale. It has the talent. It has the infrastructure foundation. It has the diplomatic position. It has the strategic autonomy that makes it the only credible third option in a bifurcated technology world. What it has not yet had is the clear-eyed accounting of what the dependency is costing, set beside a concrete vision of what the alternative looks like and what it is worth. The cost is what the previous chapters established. The alternative — and what it is worth — is where we go next.

PART FIVE

THE PRIZE

What Winning Looks Like

It is one thing to describe a cost and another to describe a prize, and arguments that only do the first tend to fail, because fear is a poor motivator for twenty-year projects. Part Five describes the prize. It has three faces. There is the external market — three billion people who have not yet built their digital foundations and are looking for someone to build with. There is the internal return — the jobs, the foreign exchange, and the compounding productivity that come from spending at home what is currently spent abroad. And there is the thing the prize is *not*: it is not walls, not autarky, not the eviction of foreign technology. The final chapter of this part defines winning precisely, so that the decisions in Part Six have a target to aim at.

CHAPTER FIFTEEN

Three Billion People With No Stack

There are roughly three billion people on earth who are not yet full participants in the digital economy.

Many of them have phones. Many have intermittent connectivity. They use WhatsApp, they watch YouTube, some have mobile-money accounts. But they do not have the infrastructure layer that separates *using other people's platforms* from *building on your own foundation*: the identity system, the payment rails, the data-governance framework, the cloud that lets domestic companies build domestic products rather than distribute foreign ones. They are in Sub-Saharan Africa, in Southeast Asia, in Central Asia, the Pacific, and parts of Latin America. They are the nations that have not yet built their digital foundations — and, almost entirely, the nations that cannot yet afford to build them without help.

They are building anyway, or trying to, with whatever tools are available — which means primarily American platforms and Chinese infrastructure.

Africa is the clearest case. The Chinese presence in African digital infrastructure is substantial and growing. Huawei has built a significant share of the mobile-network infrastructure across Sub-Saharan Africa. Transsion Holdings, a Chinese company most people outside Africa have never heard of, manufactures the majority of smartphones sold on the continent, under the Tecno, Itel, and Infinix brands; the phones Africans use to reach the internet are, in the majority, Chinese-made, running on networks that are, in significant part, Chinese-built. The American presence sits at the platform layer: Facebook is so dominant across much of Sub-Saharan Africa that many users treat "Facebook" and "the internet" as synonyms; Google dominates search; American cloud providers serve the growing enterprise market through data centres in South Africa and Kenya.

Neither the Chinese infrastructure layer nor the American platform layer was chosen by African governments in any systematic, informed way. They were chosen by default — the Chinese because they were willing to build in markets American companies judged insufficiently profitable, the American platforms because they arrived first and built network effects before any alternative existed. The sovereignty implications are understood by African governments and addressed by nothing currently available to them. The preference for a third option is explicit in the diplomatic conversations African leaders have had with Indian counterparts. India has not yet offered them anything concrete.

Southeast Asia tells a parallel story at a different income level — seven hundred million people at varying stages of digitalization, with several governments actively wary of over-dependence on either great power and openly interested in Indian digital public goods, especially after watching UPI work at scale next door.

The size of the market India is not yet serving is, by any reasonable estimate, the largest technology-market opportunity remaining in the world. Africa has 1.4 billion people today, growing toward 2.5 billion by 2050. Southeast Asia adds seven hundred million; Central Asia, the Pacific, and parts of Latin America several hundred million more. The economic value —

measured as recurring revenue from digital infrastructure over a twenty-year horizon — runs into the tens of trillions of dollars. That is not a precise estimate; it is an order of magnitude, and the point of an order of magnitude is that the precise figure does not change the conclusion. The market is very large, and India is not currently competing for it in any organized way.

What would competing require? Domestic digital infrastructure good enough to export. That infrastructure packaged so it can be deployed in countries with different languages, regulations, and technical capacity. A financing mechanism that makes Indian digital infrastructure competitive with Chinese financing terms — which is the genuinely hard part, and the subject of Chapter Seventeen. And, above all, the decision to *do* it — to name the export of digital infrastructure as a national priority with the same institutional seriousness India brought to pharmaceuticals and software services. The pharmaceutical export machine that made India "the pharmacy of the world" did not emerge spontaneously; it was the product of deliberate policy, investment in manufacturing capacity, regulatory frameworks, and sustained diplomatic engagement over decades. Digital infrastructure can follow the same path, and the path is already partly cleared by UPI's international agreements. The market is there: three billion people without a stack. The question is whether India builds one they can use, before someone else finishes building one they cannot leave.

CHAPTER SIXTEEN

What Stays in India

There is a version of the argument for building India's sovereign stack made entirely in the language of strategic necessity — the jurisdiction risk, the data-sovereignty concern, the geopolitical exposure. It is a valid argument; this book has made it across several chapters. There is another version of the same argument, made in the language of economic opportunity, that is heard less often and is arguably more powerful: building the sovereign stack is not a cost to be borne for the sake of security. It is the largest domestic job-creation and economic-circulation opportunity India has available. This chapter makes that argument with numbers, and invites the reader to challenge each one — the working is in Appendix A.

Begin with the baseline. The thirty-three billion dollars that leaves India each year does not merely leave. It leaves without generating the economic activity that the same money would generate if spent at home. When Arjun pays forty-two lakhs a year to AWS, that money pays American engineers, American real estate, American shareholders, American taxes; the economic *multiplier* — the additional activity each rupee sets off as it circulates — accrues in the United States. If Arjun paid the same forty-two lakhs to an Indian cloud provider, the money would pay Indian engineers, Indian landlords, Indian electricity bills, Indian vendors, Indian taxes, and recirculate through the Indian economy at each step. Economists estimate the domestic multiplier for technology spending in a developing economy at between 1.5 and 2.5 — meaning each rupee spent domestically generates one and a half to two and a half rupees of total activity. The difference between a rupee spent on AWS and a rupee spent on an Indian provider is therefore not one rupee. It is the multiplier. Across the total technology spending that currently flows out of India, the domestic activity *forgone* by spending abroad rather than at home is somewhere between fifty thousand crore and one lakh crore rupees a year. Every year.

Now build the employment estimate from the ground up. A domestic cloud provider serving India's current enterprise and startup market would employ differently from a foreign subsidiary: the infrastructure engineering, product development, research, management, sales, support, finance, and legal would all be in India. A provider at the necessary scale would directly employ somewhere between fifty thousand and one hundred thousand people, and these are not low-wage jobs — cloud-infrastructure engineering is among the highest-compensated technical work in the economy, with Indian compensation running between fifteen and forty lakh rupees a year depending on seniority. The direct wage bill for a domestic industry of that scale would be between seventy-five thousand crore and four lakh crore rupees a year, circulating inside India. The indirect employment is larger still: every direct technology job supports roughly three to four jobs in the surrounding economy — the housing, food, transport, education, and healthcare a well-paid technical workforce demands. A domestic cloud industry employing a hundred thousand directly generates three to four hundred thousand indirectly. And this is one sector. Apply the same logic to the social, software-subscription, and AI-development layers, and the aggregate direct employment in a fully domestic Indian stack — built to serve India's *current* digital economy, not some hypothetical future one — is between half a million and a million technical and professional jobs, with indirect employment of one and a half to four million. These are not aspirational figures plucked from optimism; they are constructed from the employment profiles of comparable foreign companies, adjusted for Indian wages and the actual mix of technical and non-technical roles technology companies generate.

Now the foreign-exchange dimension. India's foreign-exchange reserves measure its ability to manage external obligations — to service debt, stabilize the rupee, and weather shocks. The thirty-three-billion-dollar technology outflow sits on the negative side of that ledger, a current-account drain that partly offsets the celebrated IT-export surplus. Every dollar of technology spending redirected from foreign to domestic providers improves the current account by a dollar — not through increased exports, but through decreased imports. If India builds domestic alternatives that capture half of the current foreign technology spend over a decade — a conservative and achievable target given the precedents of Chapter Ten — the annual current-account improvement is on the order of sixteen billion dollars, roughly half of India's annual trade deficit. Accumulated over ten years, that is a hundred to two hundred billion dollars added to India's external buffer. Against reserves that stood around six hundred and ninety billion dollars in late 2025, that is a fifteen-to-thirty-per-cent improvement in external resilience — without a single new export, without additional currency risk, simply by spending at home what is currently spent abroad.

There is one more dimension, and it is the one that compounds. Technology companies are not only employers; they are infrastructure. The cloud provider that hosts Indian startups determines what tools those startups can reach. The AI infrastructure Indian developers can access determines what Indian applications can do. A domestic technology-infrastructure sector does not merely employ people — it raises the productivity of every *other* sector of the economy. Agricultural technology built on Indian data by Indian developers on Indian compute will serve Indian farmers better than technology built on the same data by foreign developers for a global market. Healthcare AI trained on Indian patient data by Indian researchers will be more accurate for Indian patients than systems trained on Western populations. The agricultural GDP that grows because farmers have better tools, the healthcare cost that falls because diagnosis is more accurate, the credit that flows because Indian fintech understands Indian financial behaviour — all of that is additional, and all of it compounds.

So the thirty billion dollars that leaves India every year is not just money. It is the investment that is *not* being made in the productivity of the Indian economy. Redirecting it does not merely save thirty billion dollars; it generates the multiplied, compounding activity of a technology sector building for India, on Indian foundations, with Indian resources.

Arjun's AWS bill arrives on the third of each month. Forty-two lakhs, settled in dollars; the engineering salaries, the real estate, the vendor relationships, the taxes — all of it happening in Seattle. Imagine, for a moment, that it happened in Bengaluru instead. Multiply Arjun by eighty thousand Indian startups. Add the enterprises, the government, the schools, the hospitals. Add the compounding effect of engineers paid Indian wages spending those wages in Indian cities. Add the foreign exchange that accumulates rather than drains. Add the infrastructure layer that makes the next generation of Indian companies better than this one. The number is not thirty billion dollars. It is several times that — denominated in rupees, and staying in India.

CHAPTER SEVENTEEN

The Third Option

This is what winning looks like.

Not the elimination of foreign technology. Not walls. Not a return to the License Raj in digital form, where Indian companies are protected from competition regardless of whether they deserve to win. Not nationalism as an end in itself, substituting Indian mediocrity for foreign excellence on the grounds of origin. Any of those would betray the very users — Priya, Arjun, Suman — in whose name the argument is made, because all three of them deserve tools that are good, and a worse tool with an Indian flag on it is still a worse tool.

Winning looks like this: Indian digital infrastructure that is good enough to choose on its merits, governed by Indian law, building capability that compounds inside India, and available to the world as a genuine alternative to the two options it currently has. It is a specific vision, and it requires specific things to be true.

The first is that the *public infrastructure layer gets completed.* India built the payments layer; UPI works, and it needs to be extended internationally at pace. India built the identity layer; Aadhaar works, and its privacy architecture needs to keep improving. What India has not yet built at the required scale is the *compute* layer. The cloud infrastructure that Indian companies can run on without leaving Indian legal jurisdiction does not yet exist in a form competitive with AWS, Azure, or Google Cloud. Building it is the central infrastructure task of the next decade — the missing rail without which every other layer remains a tenant on someone else's land.

The second is that the *data layer gets governed* — not merely for privacy, but as an economic resource. The DPDP Act has to evolve from a privacy framework into a data-governance framework that addresses the economic dimension: who can collect what data, on what consent terms, for what purposes, with what obligation to share value with the people who generated it. The specific instrument that deserves serious attention is a *data-dividend mechanism*: a framework under which foreign platforms that extract economic value from Indian user data contribute to a domestic AI-development fund, whose proceeds build Indian AI infrastructure on Indian data. The contribution would not be punitive; it would be proportional to the value extracted, on a methodology the platforms themselves could audit. It converts an uncounted, uncompensated outflow into a measured, reinvested one — the invoice of Chapter Five, finally sent.

The third is that the *talent stays, or returns.* The three hundred thousand engineers who leave each year are not permanently lost; many will return, or want to, if the conditions at home make return the rational choice. And the conditions that matter are not primarily compensation — they are the quality of the problems and the quality of the infrastructure. India is the most complex technical environment on earth, and solving for India means solving for a scale and diversity no other environment offers. Making that argument credibly, and backing it with the infrastructure that makes it true, is the strategy for retaining and attracting the talent the sovereign stack requires. The diaspora does not need to be repatriated. It needs to be oriented.

The fourth is that the *export develops from a vision into a business.* The three billion people without a stack are not waiting indefinitely; infrastructure decisions are being made right now, in every capital in Sub-Saharan Africa and Southeast Asia, about what to build on. India has a window measured in years, not decades, to establish the relationships, the financing, and the technical packages that would make Indian digital infrastructure the default choice for nations that do not want to choose between Washington and Beijing. The financing is the hardest part. Chinese infrastructure investment across Africa has run on concessional loans, favourable terms, and a willingness to build where commercial capital will not go — terms Indian government finance has not yet matched. The Exim Bank, the development-finance institutions, the Lines of Credit India already uses for *physical* infrastructure abroad need to be explicitly extended to digital infrastructure, with the same urgency and at the same scale.

The fifth thing that must be true is the one all the others depend on: *India decides.* The dependency did not grow from a decision. It grew from the *absence* of a decision — from a billion individual choices, each rational, whose aggregate produced a structure no one intended and no one chose. The solution requires what the problem did not: deliberate collective choice. The choice is not complicated in its essence, though it is complex in execution. It is the choice to treat digital infrastructure as a national priority in the same category as physical infrastructure, defence capability, and food security — as something whose provision cannot be left entirely to the market, because the national interest in having it is not fully captured by the market returns it generates. India has made this choice before, in each of those domains. It built roads and power plants and ports through public investment when private capital would not go. It maintained defence-manufacturing capability when commercial logic would have outsourced it. It held strategic food reserves through public procurement when the market would have sold them off. Digital infrastructure is the infrastructure of the twenty-first century in the same way roads were the infrastructure of the twentieth. The choice to build it, or to keep borrowing it, is the defining infrastructure choice of this generation.

The choice is available. The capability exists. The market opportunity is there. The geopolitical window is open. What remains is the decision.

Priya takes the bus home from school at four-thirty. She opens Instagram at the bus stop, the way she does most days, because the nine minutes between the end of school and the arrival of the bus are hers, and she has learned to use them. She scrolls — a cousin's child's first steps, a recipe she will consider and probably not make, a reel that makes her smile. She does not think about the forty-two rupees. But somewhere in a ministry in Delhi, someone is reading a document that has added up all the forty-two rupees, across all the Priyas, across all the mornings, and arrived at a number that requires a response. This book is that document. What happens next is a choice.

PART SIX

THE CHOICE

Everything to this point has been diagnosis and possibility. Part Six is prescription. A structural problem, however large, eventually resolves into a finite set of discrete decisions that either get made or do not. This part names them — fifteen of them, sorted by how long they take to mature, each stated honestly enough to include the objection it will face. Then it does the one thing a book like this owes its reader: it shows, in two plain extrapolations of the year 2047, what India becomes depending on whether the decisions are made. And it ends not with the policymaker but with the reader — because the choice is not only Delhi's.

CHAPTER EIGHTEEN

Fifteen Decisions

Every large structural problem resolves, at some point, into a set of discrete decisions that either get made or do not. The dependency this book describes did not emerge from a single failure, and it will not be resolved by a single intervention. It will be resolved, if it is resolved, by a sequence of specific choices, made by specific institutions, within specific windows, that collectively change the conditions inside which the next Arjun and the next Priya and the next Suman operate.

This chapter names fifteen of them, across three horizons. They are framed as *choices* rather than recommendations, because the honest description of each includes its cost and its strongest objection. A recommendation that cannot survive its own counter-argument is not worth making.

The Immediate Horizon: decisions for the next two years

Decision One — Publish the accounting. The most basic decision, and the one that makes the others possible, is to turn the thirty-three-billion-dollar outflow into a number that appears in India's official economic accounting. The Ministry of Finance should commission and publish an annual *Digital Balance of Payments* — a systematic accounting of the flows of Chapters Four and Five, updated yearly, disaggregated by category, with methodology stated and sources cited. The cost is essentially nil; it is a research and publication exercise. *Objection:* "Publishing the number invites alarmism and antagonizes partners." *Response:* The number is already discoverable by anyone who looks; the choice is only whether India measures it deliberately or is told it later by someone else. You cannot govern what you refuse to count.

Decision Two — Extend procurement preference to domestic cloud. Government technology procurement runs to several thousand crore rupees a year. A policy requiring agencies to evaluate domestic cloud providers first — not to use them regardless of quality, but to justify in writing any decision to choose a foreign provider over a qualified domestic alternative — would create the captive early market that Chapter Ten identified as the engine of Korea's industrialization. A domestic provider meeting eighty per cent of the specification at a comparable price should win. *Objection:* "This protects mediocrity." *Response:* The eighty-per-cent-and-comparable-price bar is the safeguard; below it, the foreign provider still wins. Procurement guarantees a market, not a pass.

Decision Three — Establish the National Data Endowment. The data-dividend mechanism of Chapter Seventeen needs an institutional home. A National Data Endowment — a public institution at arm's length from government, funded by a levy of two to three per cent on foreign-platform revenue derived from Indian user data — would supply both the architecture and the funding for domestic AI development, disbursed through competitive grants to

Indian researchers and startups working on Indian-data, Indian-problem applications. *Objection:* "This is a tax that will be passed to consumers or invite retaliation." *Response:* Set proportionate to value demonstrably extracted and made auditable by the platforms themselves, it is a royalty on a resource, not a penalty — and the proceeds rebuild the very capability the extraction erodes.

Decision Four — Pass the Data Portability Right. The DPDP Act establishes consent for collection; it does not yet establish the right of Indian users to *take their data with them* — to download their behavioural history, content, and social graph and move it to a competitor or a domestic alternative. The EU's Digital Markets Act requires this of large platforms; India should require it of all platforms above a user threshold. *Objection:* "Portability is technically burdensome and rarely used." *Response:* Its value is structural, not statistical: it lowers the switching cost of Chapter Six, which is the single mechanism holding the lock-in in place. It need not be used often to matter; it needs only to exist.

Decision Five — Create the Digital Infrastructure Investment Fund. A dedicated fund, capitalized at a minimum of fifty thousand crore rupees over five years, would supply the patient capital private markets will not provide at this stage. It should not build and operate cloud infrastructure itself; it should invest in private companies building it — equity, concessional debt — in exchange for Indian data-sovereignty guarantees and competitive domestic pricing. The model is the semiconductor funds created by the United States CHIPS Act. *Objection:* "The state is a poor venture capitalist." *Response:* True, which is why the fund invests in private builders rather than operating infrastructure; its job is to correct a market timing failure, not to pick winners forever.

The Medium Horizon: decisions for three to seven years

Decision Six — Build the sovereign AI compute cluster. India needs, within five years, a national AI compute facility on the model of its national nuclear and space facilities: at minimum on the order of a hundred thousand high-end AI training accelerators, operated as shared national infrastructure, open to Indian researchers and companies on competitive access terms, priced to make Indian AI development feasible for startups and universities. *Objection:* "Hardware ages; this is a depreciating bet." *Response:* So is every road and every power station; strategic infrastructure is renewed, not avoided, and the alternative is renting all national AI capacity from abroad in perpetuity.

Decision Seven — Mandate ONDC adoption for government digital services. ONDC has the architecture right; it needs the scale only mandated adoption can supply in the medium term. Requiring all government-run digital marketplaces and procurement platforms to implement ONDC protocols would provide both the transaction volume and the engineering pressure to mature the network to the point where private adoption becomes rational. *Objection:* "Mandates entrench an unproven standard." *Response:* The standard is open and non-proprietary; mandating an open protocol is the opposite of entrenching a private one, and is exactly how UPI reached escape velocity.

Decision Eight — Launch the India Digital Infrastructure Export Agency. A dedicated agency, modelled on the institutions that exported Indian pharmaceutical and physical-infrastructure capability, would package Indian digital infrastructure for partner countries, coordinate with the Exim Bank on concessional financing, provide technical assistance to partner governments, and maintain the relationships that make India a credible alternative to Chinese and American technology partnerships. *Objection:* "India should fix its own gaps before exporting." *Response:* The export market funds the domestic build; waiting for perfection at home cedes the window abroad to China, and the two efforts reinforce rather than compete with each other.

Decision Nine — Reorient engineering education and research toward sovereign-stack priorities. Incorporating digital sovereignty, Indian data governance, and Indian AI priorities into the standard curriculum at the IITs and NITs signals to those weighing whether to stay that the problems at home merit the same intellectual engagement as the problems abroad. The more important reform is research funding: redirecting public research money toward sovereign-stack problems — agricultural AI, healthcare AI, Indian-language models — changes what the best Indian researchers spend their lives on. *Objection:* "Government direction distorts science." *Response:* Public funding already directs research; the only question is toward whose problems. Pointing it at India's is not distortion — it is alignment.

Decision Ten — Negotiate bilateral data-governance agreements. The CLOUD Act exposure of Chapter Seven cannot be fixed unilaterally. It requires negotiating with the United States an agreement that establishes Indian law as the governing framework for Indian user data. These negotiations are long and involve trade-offs across the relationship, which is exactly why they should begin now — the alternative, accepting indefinite foreign jurisdiction as a background condition, compounds with every year of delay. *Objection:* "This is a hard ask that could sour a good relationship." *Response:* Mature relationships survive hard asks; it is dependency, not negotiation, that strains them over time.

The Long Horizon: decisions for a decade or more

Decision Eleven — Build Indian semiconductor *design* capability. India cannot, within any realistic horizon, build leading-edge fabrication. What it can build within a decade is exceptional semiconductor *design* capability — and design is where the intellectual value, and therefore the IP revenue, is created. A nation that designs chips and fabricates them elsewhere captures the design value and accepts dependence only at the fabrication layer. *Objection:* "Design without fabrication is still dependence." *Response:* It is *bounded* dependence at the commodity layer while capturing the high-value layer — precisely the trade the most successful chip economies already make.

Decision Twelve — Develop Indian large language models on Indian data. The foundation models that will underlie most AI applications over the next decade are being trained now, on datasets assembled now. A model trained on Indian data, in Indian languages, for Indian applications would not beat GPT or Gemini on general English benchmarks — and would not need to. It would be the best model in the world for Indian uses, because it would know what a farmer in Ludhiana means by *yellowing at the stem* and what a clause of the Indian Contract Act implies. For Indian users in Indian contexts, best-in-the-world is sufficient to win. *Objection:* "India cannot out-spend the frontier labs." *Response:* It does not have to; it has to out-*localize* them, on data they cannot obtain, for a market they treat as an afterthought.

Decision Thirteen — Complete the Digital Public Infrastructure stack. The DPI layer covers payments, identity, financial-data portability, and open commerce. It does not yet cover health data, agricultural data, educational credentials, or the data of the hundreds of millions in the informal economy. Extending the proven DPI logic to each domain would complete the foundational architecture of a sovereign digital economy. *Objection:* "Each new domain is a fresh privacy risk." *Response:* True — which is why the consent-based, distributed Account

Aggregator architecture, not a central database, is the template; the risk is managed by design, as Estonia showed.

Decision Fourteen — Build Indian digital infrastructure for the Global South. The export agenda requires, over a decade, the capacity to deploy Indian digital infrastructure across fifty or more partner countries — not just shipping technology but training the local engineers who will run it, building the legal frameworks that govern it in each jurisdiction, and sustaining the diplomatic relationships that make it a trusted choice. This is the work of a generation, on the model that built the pharmaceutical export industry. *Objection:* "This is expensive generosity." *Response:* It is not generosity; it is market creation, relationship capital, and standards leadership — the same logic that made Indian pharma a strategic asset, not a charity.

Decision Fifteen — Choose. The fifteenth decision is not a policy instrument. It is the prior commitment without which the other fourteen are gestures: the decision, made at the level of national political leadership, to treat digital sovereignty as a strategic priority in the same category as physical security and economic development — not as a technology-sector concern, not as a privacy matter, but as a foundational question about what kind of economy and what kind of nation India is building for the next century. Every nation that has addressed a comparable dependency did so because it was named, at the highest level of authority, as something that required addressing. India has made commitments of this kind before, on problems of comparable complexity, and followed through: the nuclear program, the space program, the green revolution, UPI. Digital sovereignty is the infrastructure problem of this generation. The decision is available. *Objection:* "There is no political constituency for an abstraction." *Response:* There was none for nuclear self-reliance or for UPI either, until leadership made the abstraction concrete. Constituencies follow commitments; they rarely precede them.

CHAPTER NINETEEN

Two Versions of 2047

India will be one hundred years old as an independent nation in August 2047. The centenary has already become a planning horizon — a target date for economic and social goals across every domain of national development. India at 2047 is the frame for long-range thinking in Delhi and in every state capital.

This is the chapter about what *digital* India looks like at one hundred, in two versions. The first happens if the decisions of Chapter Eighteen are not made, or made too slowly and too partially to matter. The second happens if they are made well and sustained over the twenty years between now and then. Neither is a prediction. They are extrapolations — honest extensions of trajectories visible now, carried forward twenty years with the compound effects that time and consistency produce.

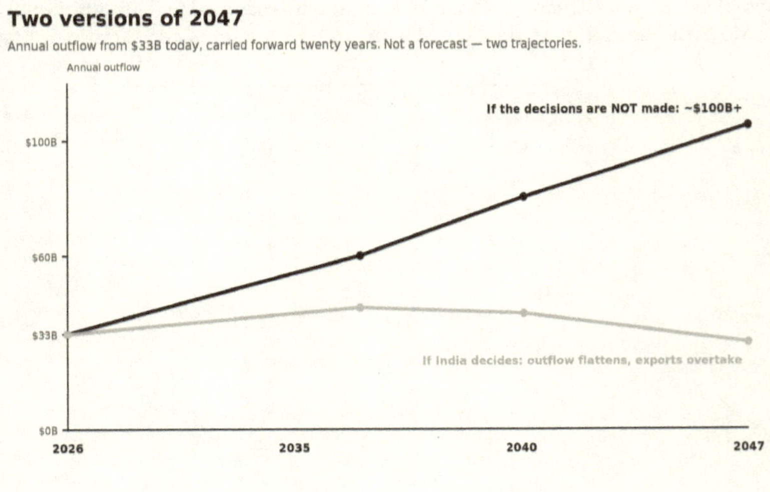

Figure 10. Extrapolation of trajectories in Chapter 19, not a prediction

The First Version

In the first version, the decisions are not made. Not entirely — India is too large and too dynamic for nothing to happen. Some domestic cloud infrastructure is built. Some AI investment occurs. Some of the fifteen decisions are partially implemented. But the urgency is not there, the coordination is not there, and the sustained political commitment is not there. The window that exists in 2026 — before the AI infrastructure market is fully consolidated, before the switching costs compound further — closes without India filling it.

By 2035, the artificial-intelligence layer of the global economy is substantially consolidated. Three or four American foundation-model providers, with one or two Chinese competitors, supply the AI infrastructure on which most of the world's applications run. Indian companies build on top of these models, paying for access, subject to foreign terms of service, generating revenue that accrues outside India. The data Suman's agricultural queries contributed to — along with the queries of a hundred million Indian farmers over the decade from 2020 to 2030 — is now embedded in a foreign foundation model that Indian agricultural-extension services pay three lakh rupees a year, per district, to access through an API. The intelligence was built from Indian knowledge. The product is sold back to India. The price was set in California.

By 2040, the foreign-exchange outflow has grown from thirty-three billion dollars toward something closer to a hundred billion. The AI layer has added its costs to the existing cloud, social, and software outflows, and as the Indian economy has grown its technology spending has grown with it. The current-account deficit is structurally larger than it would have been, requiring more foreign borrowing to finance and deepening India's external vulnerability. The Global South infrastructure choices have been made: the fifty countries for which India was the natural partner have built on Chinese infrastructure, because the Chinese offer was there and the Indian offer was not developed or financed enough to compete. The diplomatic relationships that would have followed Indian infrastructure into those countries never formed.

India in 2047 is a large, sophisticated, growing economy with a capable technology sector. It is also an economy whose digital layer is substantially rented from foreign providers, whose data is governed by foreign law, whose AI infrastructure is controlled by foreign companies, and whose technology spending is a permanent structural drain on the current account. It is not a disaster — India is resilient. But it is not what India could have been. It is a tenant in its own digital house, paying rent that rises every year, on a lease it cannot read and did not sign.

The Second Version

In the second version, the decisions are made. Not perfectly — no undertaking of this scope is implemented without error, revision, and setback. But the core commitments are made, the institutional machinery is built, and the twenty-year trajectory is established within the first five years, so the compound effects have time to accumulate.

By 2030, the National Data Endowment is operational and has disbursed its first generation of grants to Indian AI developers. The sovereign AI compute cluster has its first phase of hardware running. Three or four Indian cloud providers have reached the scale to serve enterprise customers competitively, funded in part by the government procurement preference that gave them their first market.

By 2035, the AI layer looks different. India has foundation models trained on Indian data, in Indian languages, for Indian applications — the most capable models available for Indian agriculture, Indian legal work, Indian healthcare, Indian languages. Suman's son Kulwant, now working for an Indian agritech company in Chandigarh, uses a tool built on a model trained in part on queries from farmers like his father. The intelligence stays in India. The price is set in India. The revenue goes to an Indian company that employs Indian engineers. The export agenda is generating returns: thirty-five countries have deployed Indian digital infrastructure at some layer — UPI-based payments here, Aadhaar-model identity there, ONDC-based commerce elsewhere — and Indian technology companies are following the public infrastructure into those markets, building the application layers on top, exactly as private Indian firms built payment apps on top of UPI.

By 2040, the foreign-exchange picture has turned. The technology outflow is still real — some dependence on foreign technology will remain permanently, and that is fine — but it has grown more slowly than in the first version, while technology *export* revenue has grown faster, and the two lines have crossed.

In 2047, at the centenary, India is something no developing nation has previously been: a full-stack technology power. Not by owning the most powerful models or the most valuable platforms, but by running a digital economy substantially on its own infrastructure, governed by its own law, built on its own data, and offering the world an alternative that reflects its own values and its own interests.

Priya opens Instagram at 7:14 in the morning. She still uses it; the platform still exists and is still good; the algorithm still knows she lingers longer on the dancing children than on the kajal; the forty-two rupees still flows — some of it. But not all of it. Because now there is also an Indian platform her daughter uses, one Priya does not fully understand, built by an engineer who grew up in a town not unlike Coimbatore, trained at an NIT, and stayed in India because the problem she wanted to solve was here and the infrastructure to solve it had finally been built. The platform is not better than Instagram in every way. It is better in some: it understands Tamil humour, it knows what a saree is, it does not advertise things priced for a market Priya does not live in. The forty-two rupees that does not go to Delaware goes instead to a company in Chennai that pays Indian engineers Indian salaries that circulate in Indian cities that build Indian tax revenues that fund the schools where Priya teaches. She does not know this either. But it is happening. And this time, someone is counting.

CONCLUSION

What to Do on Monday Morning

A book that ends at the centenary risks leaving the reader admiring a horizon she cannot touch. So this last page is shorter and nearer. The choice this book describes is made at the level of national leadership — but it is not *only* made there, and the reader who closes the book persuaded should know what persuasion is good for on a Monday morning.

If you are a **citizen**, the contribution is not to delete your apps; they are good, and martyrdom is not a policy. It is to stop treating the outflow as weather. Ask the question that no one in Arjun's boardroom asked: *where does the money go, and under whose law does my data live?* A public that asks that question of its representatives, its employers, and its institutions creates the constituency that Decision Fifteen requires and currently lacks.

If you are a **founder or an engineer**, the contribution is the orientation of Chapter Thirteen. You do not have to move home or take a pay cut. You have to point the most interesting years of your career at the most interesting problems on earth, which happen to be Indian — and, when a credible domestic option exists, to choose it, and when it does not yet exist, to consider building it.

If you are a **policymaker or an investor**, the fifteen decisions of Chapter Eighteen are the agenda, and the first one costs almost nothing: publish the accounting. Everything else becomes arguable the moment the number is official.

The dependency grew from the absence of a decision — from a billion rational choices that added up to a structure no one chose. It is the rare large problem whose origin is also its remedy: what was built by the absence of choice can be unbuilt by the presence of one. The number is now counted. The models have been studied. The advantages have been inventoried. The window is open, and it is open for years, not decades.

What happens next is a choice. It always was.

THE LEDGER

The receipts, the sources, and the gratitude

AUTHOR'S NOTE

The numbers in this book are honest numbers. They are ranges, not points, because honest uncertainty is more useful than false precision. They are constructed from corporate disclosures, industry research, government publications, and the first digital balance-of-payments analysis Peaqlabs has produced. The full methodology, source documentation, and data tables appear in Appendix A and in the accompanying research paper at the Peaqlabs website.

The three people who open this book and recur through it — Priya, Arjun, and Suman — are composites. Their specific details are invented; their situations are real. There are hundreds of millions of Priyas, tens of thousands of Arjuns, and hundreds of millions of Sumans, and every decision they make in these pages is one their circumstances made rational. This book has no argument with any of them.

Its argument is with the structure. And the structure can be changed.

Sivakumar Gingee Peaqlabs, 2026

APPENDIX A

India's Digital Balance of Payments — Methodology and Tables

This appendix exists so that the central claim of the book — that India transfers a conservative floor of roughly thirty-three billion dollars a year to foreign technology companies, plus an estimated ten to thirty billion dollars a year in unpriced data value — can be checked rather than believed. It states the method, the sources, and the known limitations. Where a figure is an estimate, it is labelled an estimate. Where the data is weak, the appendix says so.

A.1 Method and principles

Four principles govern the construction.

1. **Ranges, not points.** Each category is presented as a low–high band built from at least two independent sources where available. The headline "$33 billion" is the sum of the *low* estimates across all seven categories — a deliberate floor, not a midpoint.
2. **Conservative on data.** Category Seven (data) is the largest and least certain. The book uses its low estimate ($10bn) in the headline floor and reports the full $10–30bn band separately, so a reader who rejects the data estimate entirely can still work with a ~$23bn floor across Categories One–Six.
3. **Outflow, not gross spend.** The figures attempt to capture the value accruing to *foreign* parent entities, not total Indian spend on a category (which includes domestic salaries, resellers, and taxes that stay in India).
4. **Stated sources, stated gaps.** Every category cites the class of source used and notes where official data does not exist and estimation was required.

A.2 Category construction

#	Category	Low–High (USD/yr)	Primary basis	Confidence
1	Social media & search advertising	$7–9 bn	Meta & Alphabet India revenue (regional disclosures + analyst estimates); Indian digital-ad market reports	Medium-high

#	Category	Low–High (USD/yr)	Primary basis	Confidence
2	Cloud infrastructure	\$6–8 bn	India cloud-market size (analyst firms) × foreign hyperscaler share (AWS/Azure/GCP)	Medium-high
3	Software subscriptions	\$3–5 bn	Enterprise SaaS spend (Microsoft 365, Adobe, Salesforce, Zoom, etc.) from vendor disclosures + market reports	Medium
4	App-store commissions	\$1–2 bn	Android/iOS in-app purchase volume × 15–30% commission	Medium
5	Digital-payments fees	\$0.8–1.5 bn	Cross-border card/SWIFT/processor fees on India's international digital commerce	Low-medium
6	Hardware & semiconductor IP	\$5–8 bn	IP/royalty component of India's electronics & semiconductor import bill	Low-medium
7	Data (unpriced)	\$10–30 bn	Implied training-data value; see A.3	Low (intentionally conservative)
	Floor (sum of lows)	**≈ \$33 bn**		
	Midpoint (full range)	**≈ \$48 bn**		

A.3 Note on Category Seven (data)

Category Seven has no invoice, so it cannot be measured directly; it must be *imputed*. The book's low estimate is derived conservatively by reference to (a) the share of leading platforms' user base and engagement that is Indian, (b) the documented premium on diverse, multilingual training data, and (c) comparable valuations placed on data assets in technology-company disclosures and acquisitions. The $10–30bn band is wide on purpose. The honest position is that the true figure is unknown because no institution with the authority to compel disclosure has asked for it — which is itself the argument of Chapter Five. Readers who prefer to exclude Category Seven entirely are invited to do so; the Categories One–Six floor of roughly $23bn is sufficient to carry the book's argument.

A.4 Reference points used in the text (current as of 2026)

- India's software & IT-services **exports:** ≈ **US$205 billion** in FY2024-25 (RBI survey basis; MeitY reports a higher figure on a broader basis). *This is the surplus the book contrasts with the uncounted outflow.*
- **UPI** volume: on the order of **185 billion transactions** in FY2024-25, exceeding the global combined transaction count of Visa and Mastercard by number; average settlement under three seconds.
- **Aadhaar** enrolment: ≈ **1.38 billion** people.
- India's **foreign-exchange reserves:** ≈ **US$690 billion** (late 2025).
- **India cloud market:** ≈ US$6–8 billion, growing 30–40% annually.

A.5 Limitations

The construction depends on company-level disclosures that are not designed to isolate India-attributable parent-company value, on third-party market sizing that varies by firm, and on imputation for the data category. The figures should be read as a first, deliberately conservative national estimate intended to make an uncounted flow *countable* — and as a standing invitation to the institutions with subpoena power and audit access to do it properly. That invitation is Decision One.

NOTES

The notes below identify the principal classes of source behind each chapter's factual claims. Full citations and live links appear in the companion research paper published by Peaqlabs.

Introduction. India IT/software-services export figure: Reserve Bank of India survey of software exports, FY2024-25 (≈US$204.7bn), and Ministry of Electronics and IT statements on IT exports. Aggregate outflow figures: see Appendix A.

Chapter 1 (7:14 AM, Coimbatore). Per-session and per-user advertising value: derived from Meta/Alphabet India revenue divided across the active Indian user base (Appendix A, Category 1). Indian social-media user base: industry estimates of ~500 million active users.

Chapter 2 (The Startup Stack). Indian startup counts: DPIIT recognition data and startup-ecosystem trackers (ranges reflect differing definitions). Cloud spend per startup and aggregate startup cloud outflow: Appendix A, Category 2. AWS pricing-change and terms-of-service characterizations: AWS Customer Agreement (public).

Chapter 3 (What the Crop Knows). Agricultural-household count: ~150 million (Agriculture Census / NABARD basis). Indian-language data scarcity and training-data value: see Chapter 5 notes and Appendix A.3.

Chapter 4 (Following the Money). All seven categories: Appendix A.2. Meta/Google India revenue: company regional disclosures and analyst estimates. India cloud-market size and growth: analyst-firm market reports.

Chapter 5 (The Invoice That Was Never Sent). DPDP Act 2023: Digital Personal Data Protection Act, 2023 (Government of India). Longitudinal-data point: platform entry dates into the Indian market (Google ~2005, Meta/Facebook ~2010). Value-added processing analogy: economic-history literature on raw-cotton export and textile import under colonial trade.

Chapter 6 (The Trap That Sets Itself). Switching costs, network effects, and lock-in: standard industrial-organization economics. Migration-cost example: illustrative, consistent with enterprise cloud-migration cost studies.

Chapter 7 (Whose Law Governs Your Data). CLOUD Act: Clarifying Lawful Overseas Use of Data Act, 2018 (US). *Microsoft Ireland* matter: *United States v. Microsoft Corp.* (mooted after the CLOUD Act). Export Administration Regulations: US Department of Commerce, Bureau of Industry and Security. ZTE: 2018 US Commerce Department denial order and subsequent settlement.

Chapter 8 (The Price of Walls). Chinese platform substitution timeline (Google 2010, Facebook 2009, etc.): widely documented. China cloud/TikTok/WeChat competitiveness: industry analysis.

Chapter 9 (Regulation Without Construction). GDPR (in force 2018) and Meta/Google fines; Digital Markets Act (in force 2023); GAIA-X (announced 2020); European Data Act (in force 2024): European Commission and regulator publications.

Chapter 10 (The Samsung Lesson). Korean semiconductor industrial policy from 1969; Samsung/SK Hynix/LG trajectory; ~20% of global semiconductor output: industry and economic-history sources. Indian precedents: nuclear and space (ISRO) program histories; UPI as public good (NPCI). UPI volume: see Appendix A.4.

Chapter 11 (One Million People Proved It). Estonia population ~1.4m; X-Road (2001); e-Estonia service statistics; 2007 cyberattacks and data-embassy response: e-Estonia and Estonian government publications. India DPI: Aadhaar, UPI, Account Aggregator (operational 2021), DigiLocker, ONDC.

Chapter 12 (The Stack That Already Works). UPI volume and settlement time; Aadhaar enrolment; DBT savings (government estimates); Account Aggregator architecture; ONDC design: NPCI, UIDAI, and government sources (Appendix A.4).

Chapter 13 (India's Most Expensive Export). Annual technical emigration (~300,000): immigration and skilled-migration data (ranges by definition). IIT per-student subsidy: institutional cost estimates. Indian-origin technology CEOs: public record.

Chapter 14 (Non-Alignment as a Product Feature). UPI international agreements (Singapore, UAE, France, Mauritius, Sri Lanka, Nepal, Bhutan): NPCI International and government announcements. Strategic-autonomy doctrine: Indian foreign-policy literature.

Chapter 15 (Three Billion People With No Stack). Huawei African network share; Transsion smartphone share; Facebook/Google dominance in Africa: industry and market reports. Population projections: UN data.

Chapter 16 (What Stays in India). Technology-spending multiplier (1.5–2.5): development-economics literature. Employment estimates: constructed from comparable-company employment profiles at Indian wage levels (Appendix A method). Forex reserves ~US$690bn (2025): RBI.

Chapters 17–19 & Conclusion. Policy instruments reference the precedents named in text (US CHIPS Act semiconductor funds; EU DMA portability; India's nuclear/space/green-revolution/UPI precedents). The 2047 scenarios are extrapolations, explicitly not predictions.

ACKNOWLEDGEMENTS

This book, like everything I have managed to do, rests on people whose names do not appear on its cover.

Family first, because everything begins there. To my father, **Krushnakkumar Gingee Bhoopalan**, and my mother, **Nagabhushanam Gingee Krushnakkumar**, who gave me my first sense of what is worth working for and the discipline to keep working for it: whatever steadiness this book has, it began with you. To my wife, **Chandhni MohanRam**, who carried more than her share while these pages were being written, and whose belief in the project never wavered even on the days mine did — thank you for the time, the patience, and the faith. And to my sons, **Dheeran Gingee** and **Logan Gingee**: this book is, in the end, an argument about the country you will inherit and the freedoms it will be your turn to keep. You are the reason the question felt urgent enough to answer.

To my friends, who listened to this argument long before it was a book — who asked the hard questions over too many cups of coffee, disagreed where they should have, and never let encouragement curdle into flattery — I am grateful for the company and the candour.

To my collaborators, who turned an idea into something that could stand up to scrutiny. To **Roshan Raghavander N**, Chief Technology Officer at Indobase.in, whose technical judgment and willingness to stress-test every claim made the work sharper and more honest. And to **Ramganesh Subramanian**, whose doctoral training in business administration brought rigor to the framing and saved me from more than one comfortable assumption. I am grateful, too, to the engineers, founders, farmers, and officials whose candid conversations shaped the composites of Priya, Arjun, and Suman, and to the colleagues at Peaqlabs who helped build the first digital balance-of-payments analysis on which the central claim rests.

And to all the individuals who helped shape me into who I am today — the teachers, mentors, and passing influences I could never fully list and could never honestly deny — my deepest thanks.

Whatever is right in these pages, I owe in large part to all of them. Whatever is wrong is mine alone.

ABOUT THE AUTHOR

Sivakumar Gingee writes on digital sovereignty, technology policy, and India's place in the global digital economy. He is the founder of Peaqlabs, where his work focuses on the economics of digital dependence and the building of practical alternatives to it.

ABOUT PEAQLABS

Peaqlabs is the research and technology venture behind this book. Its work spans the digital balance of payments, public digital infrastructure, and data governance — and the building of practical alternatives, including Indobase, India's managed PostgreSQL backend, and Adral, an AI workspace at India-local pricing. The full methodology and data tables behind this book are published at the Peaqlabs website.

www.ingramcontent.com/pod-product-compliance
Lightning Source LLC
LaVergne TN
LVHW090330210926
848480LV00004B/1364